Jenny's Angel

Thanks for helping me get this book into print. D L Dennis

A Novel

D. L. Dennis

© D.L. Dennis 2016

All rights reserved. No part of this book may be reproduced in any form whether mechanical, audio or photocopy without written permission from the publisher.

ISBN 978-0-9908393-1-6

Pacesetter Publishing
www.pacesetterpublishing.com
E-mail: dl@pacesetterpublishing.com

First Printing 2016

Printed in the United States of American

Books by D.L. Dennis

The Book of Common Sense for a Successful Life
The Witwer Files
Saint's Road
Jenny's Angel

Jenny's Angel is a heart warming story of a baby girl born with a deformed foot and left at the front gate of an orphanage in a basket when she was just a few weeks old. In spite of Jenny's traumatic beginnings, she brings happiness, hope and love to everyone around her along with unexplainable and miraculous events.

You will meet the dedicated staff of Anderson Calvary Orphanage whose mission is to create a family environment full of love for all the children in their care.

Jenny develops an unusual friendship with a mysterious, old man that no one can understand - no one except Jenny!

Angel

For He commands his angels with regard to you, to guard you wherever you go.

Psalm 91:11

Table of Contents

1.	CALVARY	1
2.	THE PUMPKIN PATCH	11
3.	ANDERSON CALVARY ORPHANAGE	18
4.	TRAGEDY STRIKES	23
5.	A HOUSE DESERTED	28
6.	THE "BIG HOUSE" RE-BORN	30
7.	A NEW BEGINNING FOR THE "BIG HOUSE"	32
8.	CALVARY PUMPKIN PATCH	36
9.	MIRACLE IN A BASKET	39
10.	JENNY	51
11.	AN ANGEL ON EARTH – THE DOCTOR	56
12.	JENNY THRIVES	62
13.	THE SHOE COBBLER	67
14.	HALLOWEEN PUMPKINS	75
15.	JENNY'S CRUTCH	82
16.	THE GARDEN	88
17.	THE "BIGS" & THE "LITTLES"	91
18.	THE FOOTBRIDGE AND THE FOREST	94
19.	THE CORNER CAFÉ	98
20.	THE OLD MAN	101
21.	CHRISTOPHER	106
22.	A COOKIE FOR CHRISTOPHER	110
23.	CHRISTOPHER'S PROMISE	118
24.	JENNY'S PLUNGE	122
25.	JENNY'S MIRACLE	128
26.	HOME AGAIN	137
27.	THE COAT	144
28.	RETURNING THE COAT	149
29.	THE MEDALLION	154
30.	ANOTHER MIRACLE	161
31.	GROWING UP	165
32.	THE PASSING YEARS	168
33.	ONE LAST VISIT	172

Jenny's Angel

D. L. Dennis

Pacesetter Publishing

Chapter 1

CALVARY

As the golden sun peaked over the horizon, the sleepy little town of Calvary was already beginning to show signs of life on the dusty streets. Long before the sun came up, you could see lights twinkling in several houses throughout the little community and in the farm houses that dotted the surrounding countryside. Many of the residents got an early start to their day whether they were going to work or not.

Calvary was a farming community with fields and farm houses of all sizes scattered across the countryside. For those individuals involved in farming, rising early during planting and harvesting seasons was a necessity, but this habit continued even during the winter months after the crops had been harvested and the fields were barren. "Sleeping in" was not in their vocabulary.

The businesses in the community fell into step with the rhythm of the farming community and opened their doors early to be available to fill the needs of the farmers. During planting and harvesting months, it might even be necessary to stay open late to repair a piece of equipment. Without the farmer's trade, most of the businesses would have a hard time keeping their doors open, and if that occurred, the little town of Calvary might cease to exist. That thought was not acceptable to anyone in Calvary. They were a close knit community and the residents, as well as those living for miles around, did everything they could to support the local businesses.

Jenny's Angel

Several vehicles, mostly trucks with mud-covered tires, could be seen creeping along slowly from all directions, heading to the main street to find the best parking place. Slow moving men clad in long sleeved plaid flannel shirts, bib overalls and work boots could be seen climbing out of their trucks and shuffling into the Corner Cafe, the most popular early morning gathering place. Some of the wives, and a few single ladies, would drop by the cafe a little later, but this early hour belonged to the men, and they preferred it that way. No one, male or female, ever discussed this ritual, and if anyone asked, the answer would be, "It's just the way it is." If someone new moved to Calvary, it did not take long for them to figure out that the early morning hour at the Corner Cafe belonged to the fellows.

The conversations were almost always enthusiastic and jovial, and opinions on a variety of subjects could be heard. Few problems were ever solved, but everyone knew that if they wanted to discuss a current event or had a problem, the Corner Cafe was the place to take it to get an opinion.

A steaming cup of hot coffee and a platter piled high with hot flaky biscuits and thick sausage gravy was the special every morning. That made up most of the orders for the men, with an egg or two added to some platters. Each time the door was opened, the smell of sausage frying escaped into the frosty morning air. Just the smell of it was enough to make your mouth water.

For the regulars, Susie, the waitress did not even ask what they wanted. The minute she saw them get out of their vehicle or come through the door, she had their cups of coffee poured in the thick white mugs and their orders put on the kitchen window counter for the cook. Sugar bowls and little pitchers of cream had been filled before the "Open" sign was hung out and were setting on the counter and tables. The coffee was strong, and you could see the steam curling upwards. These early morning customers were creatures of habit, not only with what time they got up each morning, but with what they ate for breakfast.

The Corner Cafe was not hard to find in Calvary. Ask any resident for directions, and they would tell you to look for the only restaurant on Main Street that sat on a corner. Then they might slap their knees and say with a chuckle, "That's why it's named the Corner Cafe."

The interior was cheerful and colorful with the red and white checked tablecloths made of oil cloth. Some of the tablecloths had been wiped off so many times, the red was beginning to fade, but no one really cared. As long as they were clean and the food was good, that was all that mattered. Those were two things that you could count on at the Corner Cafe.

Red and white checked curtains were strung on a metal rod and covered the bottom half of the windows that looked out over Main Street. When the wind howled outside and blew hard against the windows, the curtains swayed back and forth like they were doing a dance. The tables by the windows were not the most popular ones when it was cold outside and those curtains were dancing. The windows would steam up, or if it was bitterly cold outside, you might even see a little frost around the window sills. If you were one of the unfortunate ones and had to sit by the windows

Jenny's Angel

when that happened, you just might have to eat your meal with your coat on. That did not seem to keep people away from the Corner Cafe though.

The gray Formica counter, with its chrome bar stools and red vinyl seats, was in a horseshoe shape, which made it easy for Susie to refill everyone's coffee cup. Susie could carry a pot of hot, steaming coffee in each hand, pouring on each side as she walked up and down the center of the counter and never miss a beat in the conversation. She kept her eyes on the tables around the room. She would slide out from behind the counter and most of the time had the coffee cups refilled before anyone could raise a hand to let her know that the cup needed a refill. Everyone marveled at how Susie could greet everyone, take orders, fill coffee cups, deliver orders and never get flustered.

Susie had been serving up meals for more years than she wanted to talk about, but she loved her job, particularly during these early morning hours. She called everyone by their first name, and if a stranger walked in, they were not a stranger long. It would not be long before Susie was calling them by their first name and knew all about them.

Sometimes you could see Miss Callie's white head bobbing up and down in the kitchen as she helped Joe, the cook. Miss Callie was the owner of the Corner Cafe, and like Susie, she had been operating the Corner Cafe for more years than she wanted to remember. Even though she talked about closing it down or trying to sell it, no one believed her. Everyone knew that Miss Callie loved dishing up good food, but visiting with her customers was what kept her going. When she was not in the kitchen, she was flitting from one table to the other asking how their food was, or wanting to know about their families. Not much happened in Calvary that Miss Callie did not know about. No one knew just exactly how old Miss Callie was. When anyone hinted at wanting to know her age, her blue eyes would sparkle and with a grin on her face, she would say, "Honey, I've been around for a long, long time."

The Corner Cafe was also open for lunch and during the supper hour. Miss Callie was always threatening to close at 3:00 in the afternoon, but there was such an uproar from her customers, she could never go through with it. It was just as busy during the lunch and supper hours as it was for breakfast.

Early each morning, the specials of the day were written on a large blackboard that was attached to the wall. That was the first thing everyone looked at before they even took a seat. Sometimes people would pop into the Cafe just to look at the blackboard to see what the specials were for lunch and dinner, which varied from day to day and week to week. There was no pattern to what the daily specials were, and that is just the way Miss Callie wanted it. When she was asked why she did not run the specials the same each week, she would just chuckle and say, "If I did that, you wouldn't have to come in and look. I like to keep you guessin.'"

It was difficult to find a seat in the Corner Cafe when Miss Callie decided to have a "Ham and Beans and Cornbread Special" for 15 cents. Nobody could make sweet cornbread like Miss Callie, and she would not give the recipe out, not even to Joe, the cook. She said it was a secret

Jenny's Angel

recipe handed down from her family, and it was going to stay a secret! Some people liked to slather their cornbread with lots of sweet butter, and others liked to crumble it up in their bowl of beans. Every bowl had several chunks of succulent ham in with the beans. Joe learned early on that every pot he had needed to be filled with ham and beans, and he rarely had many helpings left over at the end of the day.

When it was pumpkin season, sometimes Miss Callie would add a piece of pumpkin pie with real whipped cream........at no extra cost to a meal, but that was never written on the blackboard. This was one of the many ways Miss Callie showed her appreciation to all of her loyal customers.

Lunch was served from 11:00 a. m. until 1:00 p. m., so if you wanted whatever the special was for that day, it was best to be there at 11:00 or shortly thereafter, particularly if it was ham and bean day. The word would spread like a wildfire. It seemed as though everyone in town would show up hoping that Miss Callie had chosen that day to add a piece of pie. She kept them guessing! Miss Callie never wanted anyone to leave the Corner Cafe disappointed, though, so if she ran out of pie, she would give everyone a big round, soft sugar cookie. Miss Callie was not as concerned with making money as she was with making people happy. Her soft sugar cookies were almost as famous as her cornbread and pumpkin pie, and it was not unusual for her to waltz around the tables handing out warm sugar cookies. She loved to bring a smile to everyone's face.

Most days, there was a lull in the middle of the morning

and afternoon, but even then there were always a few people popping in for a cup of coffee or a piece of pie. Nobody could make pies like Miss Callie. The flaky crust melted in your mouth, and she could make any kind of pie you could dream up. Her specialty was a banana cream pie with golden tipped meringue so high it almost toppled off.

Miss Callie always baked the pies in the early morning hours before the sun came up and the restaurant opened for breakfast. It was always dark when she started her pie baking, and she did not want to be disturbed.

When you saw the light shining dimly through the front windows from the kitchen, and the "Closed" sign on the door in those early morning hours, you knew that Miss Callie was rolling out pie crusts and whipping up the fillings! Unless the building was on fire, everyone knew not to disturb Miss Callie. She said that these early morning hours were her special prayer time. She could pray and bake at the same time!

Not often, but once in a while, Miss Callie would run a little late in getting started. On one of those days, Joe and Susie stayed out of her way during pie baking time. Puffs of flour would rise and the rolling pin would fly over the crusts as Miss Callie rolled them out. Bowls of various types of filling set on the counter waiting to be spooned into the crusts. The only thing Miss Callie would allow Joe or Susie to do was to take the pies out of the oven and slice them. She did not want anyone messing around with her pies! By the time the customers came trickling in, the pie case would be full and ready for the day. Rarely was a piece of pie left at the end of the supper hour. Joe always wished

Jenny's Angel

for at least one left over piece so he could eat it for breakfast the next day.

Miss Callie did not have any family in Calvary. She was not from around the area, and people wondered where she had met the young man she had married and how they ended up in Calvary. The old-timers just remembered that the two of them came to Calvary when they were quite young and were looking for work. Her husband started working for a farmer and had died in a farming accident just a few years after their marriage making her a widow at a very early age. Miss Callie did not talk about where she came from or about her family, so little was known about her past. She did not have any children so when she opened the Corner Cafe, it was her livelihood and her customers were her family.

Miss Callie loved to see the children come in with their moms and dads. As they were learning to talk, the little tykes were taught to say Aunt Callie. Miss Callie never tired of hearing the children call out her name. She always kept two big containers of vanilla and chocolate ice cream in the freezer in the back room. Many days she would give the children a dip of ice cream if they ate their meal. It did not take long for them to learn that Aunt Callie would give them ice cream IF she saw a clean plate!

Miss Callie also enjoyed having the children stop by after school, or on a hot afternoon during summer vacation. Many days, she would be handing out ice cream cones, even if the child's parents did not ever come to the Corner Cafe. Aunt Callie had a big heart and never wanted any child to feel left out.

People would ask her how she could make any money because she was always giving away something. Miss Callie would smile and her blue eyes twinkled as she told them that money was not important. All she cared about was having enough to live on and making people happy. No one could deny that she did a good job at that!

Miss Callie lived only a couple of blocks from the restaurant. Every day you could see her heading home for a rest after the lunch crowd cleared out. By that time of day, she had put in a full day at work, and she needed a little time off. She had always been fortunate in having good help like Susie so she did not worry about leaving for a little while in the afternoon. Susie and Joe's shift was over in the middle of the afternoon, but each of them had trained someone to take their place. Even though they did not have any ownership in the restaurant, they were as concerned about it as Miss Callie was. They always made sure that there was competent help to replace them when they left. Miss Callie was so grateful for their help and concern that whenever the receipts were tallied up for the week, Joe and Susie would find a few extra dollars in their pay envelopes.

Miss Callie loved being in the restaurant during the busy times so she rarely missed a day when she did not stay through the lunch hour. When she got home after the lunch, she would head for her easy chair and prop her feet up. It would not take long for her to drop into a sound sleep. She never told anyone how old she was, but with those early morning pie baking hours, she needed an afternoon rest. It was a rare day that she did not make it back for the supper hour, but every once in a while, she was just too tired.

Jenny's Angel

The Corner Cafe was always closed on Sunday. Her regular customers wanted her to stay open at least through the lunch hour, but she told them that Sunday was church day. If Miss Callie was not at church, before the day was over someone would go to her house to check on her because she never missed going to church. She did not want to make anybody work on Sunday. She wanted to give them the opportunity to go to church and spend time with their families. She knew she could make more money, but that was not what was important to her.

Chapter 2

THE PUMPKIN PATCH

The little town of Calvary was nestled between a river on one side and farms of all sizes spread throughout the countryside on the other three sides. The Calvary River was far enough away that there was no threat of it ever flooding the town. The population of Calvary had grown very little since the "Big Road," as the town folk called it, had been built. The "Big Road" by-passed Calvary so the little town struggled to keep businesses and attract new residents. Most of the residents of Calvary had little desire to be on the "Big Road" to make trips to the large cities to the north and to the south of Calvary. They were content to do all of their business in Calvary if at all possible.

The fields were lifeless and mostly barren on this blustery November day. Crops had been harvested, and all that remained were pieces of cornstalks sticking up haphazardly out of the ground. There were a few small rotting pumpkins left in the pumpkin patch down by the river. There had been a couple of hard freezes earlier in the month, and those pumpkins that had not been harvested had withered up, curling into strange looking shapes. Wild critters had chewed many of them into bizarre shapes.

Not many pumpkins were grown in the surrounding small communities because it was hard to compete with the Calvary Pumpkin Patch. Calvary was known for miles around for the perfectly shaped pumpkins that were grown in the Pumpkin Patch. It was somewhat of a status symbol to have made the trek to the Calvary Pumpkin Patch to pick out a pumpkin for your Jack-O-Lantern.

No one could explain why Calvary's pumpkins were so perfect nor could they explain why the harvest in the Calvary Pumpkin Patch was so plentiful each year. The local children thought it was a magical place. As soon as the vines began to pop through the soil, they loved to walk through the rows of vines and look to see how many blossoms had popped out since their last visit. They would squeal with delight when they spotted tiny pumpkins on the vines and loved to make numerous visits to watch them grow bigger and bigger.

No one could remember when the first pumpkin was grown in the Calvary Pumpkin Patch, but stories had been handed down through the families that a mysterious old man who lived in a rundown shanty near the forest of trees close to the river had grown the first pumpkin in a tiny patch of ground. His shanty was on a road which led off the main road into Calvary, and he was rarely, if ever, seen in town. When the old man died, he left his meager belongings and a little patch of ground covered in tangled pumpkin vines to a local church. The only grain of truth in the story that could be substantiated was that there was a small plot of ground with pumpkin vines on it left to one of the local churches. No one seemed to recall how the story about the old man originated, but no one disputed the truth of it. Even the adults loved to pass the story along and wanted to believe that Calvary's Pumpkin Patch was a special magical place. And, it did, indeed, produce an over-abundance of pumpkins year after year. They were as perfect as any that could be found for miles around the countryside.

THE PUMPKIN PATCH

    Not only did the Calvary Pumpkin Patch grow the most perfect pumpkins, it was also the site of the largest pumpkin patch for miles around. It belonged to Trinity Church, which was one of the four churches in town. No one in the church had any idea why the old man had left his little plot of ground to the church, which only added to the mystery of it all. Anyone who was involved with the pumpkin patch knew that it was a blessing. After the church became responsible for taking care of the pumpkin patch, those involved called it "God's Pumpkin Patch" because of the plentiful harvest each and every year. They believed that only God could perform such a miracle year after year. Trinity Church was easy to find because it was the only church that had a steeple with a bell in it. Every Sunday morning, that bell could be heard throughout the little community announcing that it was time to come to church. It was the responsibility of the church custodian to ring the bell, and most of the time, you would find a couple of the children tagging along after him asking to help. The custodian always let them climb the steps with him to where the rope hung down. He would put his hands up high on the rope and let them tug on the bottom of it. They would giggle as the bell tipped from side to side ringing loudly. If it was their first time, they usually would let go of the rope and hold their hands over their ears. That would be the highlight of the day. No one knew who had the most fun – the custodian or the children!

As funds became available throughout the years, the church had purchased additional land adjacent to the first little patch of ground that was given to them. After many years, the patch had grown so large that when the pumpkins were almost ready for harvest, they could be seen from far away. It

Jenny's Angel

looked like the earth had been splashed with various shades of orange with squiggly lines of curly green stripes. Even an artist could not have painted anything more beautiful than what nature did with the pumpkin patch.

Unless people were visiting relatives in Calvary, there were not a lot of new faces to be seen except during the fall months, when the pumpkins were being harvested. There was not much else in Calvary to draw visitors, but for several weeks, the Calvary businesses enjoyed the extra revenue they earned from all of the visitors. They made a special effort to be friendly and tried various ways to entice the visitors to come into their place of business. Some businesses put large banners in their window welcoming the visitors and others would give out a small souvenir or lollipops to the children. Most of the businesses in Calvary were closed on Sunday except during pumpkin harvesting time. During this period, many of them would open their doors on Sunday at noon. Sometimes the revenue the businesses took in during these fall months was as much as what they took in the rest of the year so they were happy to see the visitors rolling into town.

When the pumpkins got large enough to harvest, you could see them dotting the ground from quite a distance as you approached Calvary. The children would watch out the car window to see who would be the first one to spot the pumpkin patch and the pumpkin stand. A weathered, wooden stand stood on the side of the highway going into Calvary from which pumpkins were sold. The stand had been built and was maintained by volunteers from the church on the weekends. The church volunteers knew that not everyone wanted to tromp though the pumpkin patch

THE PUMPKIN PATCH

to pick one out, but would rather stop at a stand to buy their pumpkins. As soon as the pumpkins were ready to be picked until there were none left in the patch, there was always someone at the pumpkin stand from mid-morning to late afternoon to take your money. A volunteer would load up his truck with pumpkins from the patch and take them to the stand on Saturday and Sunday. Of course, no pumpkins could be purchased on Sunday until church was out at 11:00 a. m. Most everyone who stopped to buy their pumpkins at the stand drove on to Main Street. Buying pumpkins in Calvary was a family tradition which usually included lunch and a little shopping.

Of course, there was also a pumpkin stand at the church. Pumpkins decorated the church lawn along with a large hand painted "For Sale" sign which stood in one corner of the lawn. The children of the church were encouraged to help with selling the pumpkins at the church on Saturdays and after the service on Sunday. Most all of them were excited to help when they turned six and were allowed to help out. With pumpkins on the side of the road, at the church and in the patch, when you drove to Calvary, you never left without at least one pumpkin!

Sometimes the church pastor was approached by people from other communities asking if they could harvest a truck load of the pumpkins. The answer was always "no" no matter how much money was offered. The church had adopted the philosophy that if someone wanted a pumpkin from the Calvary Pumpkin Patch, they had to come to Calvary.

    Many pumpkins had to be picked for the pumpkin

stand and the church lot, but a large portion of the patch was always left unharvested for the youngsters (and some "oldsters") who wanted to roam through and pick out their own pumpkin. Little tykes could be seen struggling out of the patch with a pumpkin that weighed almost as much as they did. The church volunteers loved seeing the big grins on the faces of the children of all ages as they raced up and down with their parents tagging along after them. They tried to keep a few wagons available for those pumpkins that were just too big to carry.

There were always a few of the town folk who grumbled about the streets being crowded with strangers during those fall months, but most were happy to see some new faces – and the revenue they brought to Calvary. Visitors brought an air of excitement with them. It reminded some of the old timers of the days when Calvary was a thriving little boom town before the "Big Road" was built and by-passed their little metropolis. Since then, Calvary had slipped into the sleepy little town where no one was in a hurry, there was not much variation in the day, and most of the time it was not hard to find a parking place on Main Street. Life was slow and easy. Everyone seemed to know everyone, and only the young people looked forward to traveling to the "Big City" to the east as a big adventure. For many old timers in Calvary, they rarely ventured to the "Big City" – it was another world to them. But, most everyone did enjoy having the visitors in the fall. They enjoyed hearing the peals of laughter out of the children, seeing families enjoy time together and chatting with them in the restaurants and stores.

The Calvary Pumpkin Patch was quite unique in

that it was taken care of solely by volunteers, most of them individuals who attended the Trinity Church. Occasionally, even the custodian of the church could be seen working in the patch after he had finished his workday. For all of those involved, whether they were part of the church or not, working at the pumpkin patch or the pumpkin stand appeared to be a labor of love.

 Everyone was always amazed at how much money was raised each year in spite of the fact that many pumpkins were given away to families who could not afford to buy a pumpkin. It seemed like the more pumpkins the volunteers gave away, the more money they raised; the more they gave away, the better the crop was the next year. No one tried to explain it other than it was a miracle!

 When the last pumpkin was sold, or given away and the money was counted for one last time, the dollar amount earned would be written on a large piece of paper and posted in the window of the local newspaper office. The sales for the previous year would also be shown. The final count was usually done shortly after Halloween each year. On November 1st, people would start watching for that notice in the window. Even those individuals who were not directly involved with the pumpkin patch were eager to see what the final tally was. Each year the goal was to exceed what they had earned the year before, and rarely were they disappointed.

Chapter 3

ANDERSON CALVARY ORPHANAGE

Calvary did have something else that caught people's attention – an orphanage. The orphanage was not far from the river or the pumpkin patch, so those who visited the pumpkin patch could see it off in the distance. First time visitors were always very inquisitive as to how it came into being in such a small community. Calvary did not seem to be a likely place for an orphanage. They wondered where the children came from and how it stayed in operation in such a small remote community. It was rather mysterious even to those who lived in Calvary. Occasionally, curiosity got the best of some in a car filled with visitors, and they would drive down the little lane trying to get a closer look. They could only go so far, though, until they came upon a large, locked wrought iron gate which prevented them from going any closer. The grounds at the orphanage were completely surrounded by a tall wrought iron fence and were totally off limits to visitors, unless prior arrangements to be on the property had been made. Mrs. Miller was the director of the orphanage, and she was very protective of "her" children.

The structure which housed Anderson Calvary Orphanage had not originally been built to be an orphanage. The structure had been built on several acres not far from the Calvary River and was situated on a gravel side road which led off of a main road going into Calvary. It was a massive two story structure made of gray stone with four large pillars across the broad front porch. A wide set of

ANDERSON CALVARY ORPHANAGE

stairs led up to the concrete porch. Several tall windows were all across the front on the first floor with smaller ones on the second story. Some people said it looked like a colonial mansion from the Civil War era even though it was not white as were many colonial mansions. A few of the old timers in Calvary were alive when the original structure was built. Very few Calvary residents could claim that they had ever been in the structure, but when asked about it, there was always a story to be told. If you lived in Calvary for any length of time, you had heard the story many times and in a short time, considered yourself an expert. And, as stories go, it got bigger and better with each telling.

 Before the structure was turned into an orphanage, it was always referred to as the "Big House." It stood vacant for many years before being turned into the orphanage. There had been an air of mystery surrounding the "Big House" from the day the first construction truck turned down the rutted lane to the property, then while the "Big House" was being built, and throughout the time it was used as a residence. The "Big House" then stood empty for many years and interest in it died down, but was revived again when construction trucks once again bumped down the lane and a flurry of activity could be seen. The day the large white sign with bold black lettering, "Anderson Calvary Orphanage" was hung, for weeks it was the topic of conversation in the early morning hours at the Corner Cafe.

 The one fact that did not change as stories were told about the "Big House" was that it had been built on land purchased by a very wealthy couple whose last name was Anderson. This fact could not be disputed since it was in the county records. No one knew where the Andersons came from, or why they chose to purchase property in their community. Of course, lots of ideas were bantered around, but it was all speculation.

Rarely did anyone ever see Mr. or Mrs. Anderson unless they happened to be on the highway headed toward the "Big Road." When they saw a shiny black Rolls Royce headed in that direction, they knew that the Andersons were headed to the "Big City." It was certain that no one in Calvary had a car like that, so it had to be the Andersons. Neither Mr. nor Mrs. Anderson ever came into any of the stores or restaurants in Calvary. They remained a mystery for the short time that they resided in the "Big House."

On rare occasions, the gardener, or one of the household staff was seen in the local grocery store or the hardware store. Whoever came was always cordial, but did not fraternize with the town residents so no one was able to learn anything about the Andersons. Their lack of information, though, was not for lack of trying. Everyone was very curious about the Andersons and took every opportunity to ask a question or two. They just never got any answers!

Everyone who worked for the Andersons lived at the "Big House" with them. Evidently part of the house had been built for the purpose of housing the staff. Of course, no one in Calvary knew how many people were employed by the Andersons, but they did see cars occasionally leaving the property being driven by various individuals. The whole situation was very puzzling to the Calvary residents and gave them a lot to talk about. The "Big House" represented another world unknown to Calvary residents.

Even though the town residents knew very little about the "Big House" and its occupants, they were quite proud that such a wealthy couple had chosen their little town to build such an impressive structure close to it. Aside from the fall months when pumpkins were being harvested, not a lot happened in Calvary, so the Andersons and the "Big House" gave those who gathered in the Corner Cafe, and the other public places, something to chat and speculate about.

The town residents were fascinated with the entire construction process of the "Big House" from the time the first truck rolled down the lane until the last one left. Once the construction and landscaping were completed, it was truly a stunning estate, even from a distance. The spacious yard was turned into grounds that looked like a well-cared for park. Trees with broken limbs had been cut down, scraggly bushes had been removed, weeds pulled out and the ground had been smoothed over. The landscapers toiled long hours planting flowers, hedges and flowering trees and bushes which bloomed at various times of the year. From early spring when the purple Iris burst into their majestic blossoms until late fall when the buds of the mums broke out into full bloom, the yard was ablaze with color. The red Cannas that bloomed late in the summer months stood tall and regal against the gray stone and surrounded the house. Hollyhocks, with their bell shaped flowers of many colors, stood tall on one side of the wrought iron fence. Saplings of various fruit trees had been planted on the back of the property. Watching the landscape bloom at the "Big House" was like looking through a kaleidoscope with ever

Jenny's Angel

changing colors. It was worth the drive down the gravel road several times from spring through fall just to see the various blooming trees, flowers and bushes even though it was only at a distance, and the Calvary residents did just that!

Quite often, curiosity got the best of some of the locals, and they would drive down the gravel road at various times of the day and evening just to see if they could see any activity around the "Big House." Of course, they had to turn around when they got to the wrought iron gate, but one or two always came back with a story about what they saw, or thought they saw. No one ever knew for sure if any of the stories were true, or a figment of someone's imagination.

Early one morning, the Corner Cafe was abuzz with chatter about what the latest trip by the "Big House" had revealed when a local had taken a trip down the lane. If you could bring back a tidbit about the "Big House", you would be the center of attention for days. On one particular trip, a large swing set had been erected on one side of the massive yard. No children had ever been observed in the yard so why would a swing set have been built? They speculated that it must be an indication that there would be children in the "Big House" soon! Now, there was one more mysterious happening at the "Big House" for them to chat about!

Chapter 4

TRAGEDY STRIKES

As the months passed by, talk about the "Big House" died down. Nothing unusual seemed to be happening on the premises and no one ever caught more than a fleeting glance of anyone associated with it so it faded into the background of the daily happenings in Calvary. Life hummed along at its usual slow pace until just before noon one day a couple of years later when one of the local doctors received a frantic call at his office to come immediately to the "Big House." He had never been to the "Big House," nor had he ever met the residents so he was quite surprised to receive the call. He could hardly understand the person screaming on the other end of the phone line, but quickly determined it must be an emergency.

Doc grabbed his jacket, tore out of his office, jumped in his car and sped down Main Street as fast as he dared go. It was a Saturday morning so a lot of people were milling around on the sidewalks, in the stores and restaurants. Everyone could hear the car roaring down the street and the horn honking warning everyone to get out of the way. Those crossing the street hurried to get out of the way and scratched their heads. They all wondered why the doctor was in such a hurry and where he was going. Others popped out of the stores asking what was going on.

The news of Doc racing down Main Street spread through the little community as fast as fire on a dry, windy day. Little clumps of people gathered on the street corners speculating about what could have happened and to whom. Even those who were strangers in town were caught up in the speculation. A few people went about their business, but most stood around waiting to see when the doctor would return.

It was not long before the local coroner was observed speeding down Main Street in the same direction. In a small town where everyone knows everybody, and there is only one main street in and out of town, it is hard to keep anything a secret. These two unusual events had everyone scratching their heads trying to figure out what could have happened. It did not take long for the local telephone operator to spread the word that something had happened at the "Big House." There were no secrets with telephones on party lines. Evidently the doctor had not said anything when he called the coroner other than to come to the "Big House," so she had no other information.

What kind of tragedy could have occurred? Did something happen to one of the Andersons? Or, both of them? Or, maybe it was one of the hired help? Did someone die? Someone had to be dead or the coroner would not have been called, would he? Of course, no one had any answers, just a lot of questions. The telephone operator had not heard anything except that they needed a doctor immediately so their questions went un-answered.

The doctor was the first one to return to town. He did not wave to anyone on the street, nor even look in their direction as usual, but sped along Main Street as fast as he could safely do. As he parked his car in front of his office and got out, he had a strained look on his face. A couple

TRAGEDY STRIKES

of people approached him trying to find out what had happened, but he quickly brushed them off unwilling to say anything, although he knew it would be only a matter of time before the whole town would know. Once the facts were out, word would spread far and wide, quicker than snow would melt in July, but right now, he did not have any answers for the tragedy that had happened and was too distraught to speak to anyone. He needed to be alone for a few minutes to sort out his thoughts and get his emotions under control. He was overwrought at what had happened. Death was never easy to deal with, even for a doctor, but this was such a sad circumstance that he wanted to be left alone.

He knew it would be the coroner's responsibility to handle the situation after he left, but he was devastated at what had happened. He had felt totally helpless, and that was so difficult for him. After all, he was a doctor!

Thoughts rolled around in his head as the tears flowed down his ruddy cheeks. Could he have saved lives if he had gotten there earlier? Did they try to get in touch with someone else before they called him? Why had this tragedy happened? He had no answers now and knew he never would. He sat at his desk with his head on his arms and wept uncontrollably.

The coroner's trip into town was no different than the doctor's. He sped down Main Street avoiding everyone's eyes as he drove by. As he parked his car and headed to his office, he circumvented everyone's questions about what he found on his trip to the "Big House." He ducked into his office as quickly as he could move. He, too, was devastated

Jenny's Angel

by the circumstances. It was such a sad situation, and one that he had never been confronted with. As a coroner, his job was to deal with death, but this trip had upset him greatly. He was too distressed to talk with anyone at the moment. He knew he had to gather his thoughts and get them straightened out, but he was heavyhearted and needed a few minutes to be alone.

Surprisingly, not much information had leaked out, but that did not stop all of the conjecturing among the town residents about what might have taken place at the "Big House." The coroner's desk was close to his front door. In his haste to get inside, he had not gotten the door closed all of the way. He could hear the conversations of the groups huddled together on the sidewalk.

When the information finally came out about what had taken place at the "Big House," the residents of Calvary were in shock. Even though they did not know the Andersons personally, they considered them a part of their community and were saddened. When the information about the deaths appeared in the weekly newspaper a few days later, the residents of Calvary knew little more about what had happened, but what did shock them was that there were two obituaries. These obituaries gave little information except that Rochelle Anderson of Calvary died giving birth to a stillborn son and daughter and that private services were to be held in an undisclosed location. That was the extent of the information in the obituaries – one for Mrs. Anderson and one for the twins. They stated the basics and nothing more.

Little information had been garnered throughout

TRAGEDY STRIKES

the time the Andersons had occupied the "Big House," and in the death of Mrs. Anderson and the twins, little was revealed. Neither the doctor nor the coroner ever discussed what took place on that fateful day, no matter how much they were prodded with questions. When the subject was brought up, they ignored the topic or quickly made an exit. It did not take long for everyone to realize that there would be no comments coming forth from either of them.

After the tragedy at the "Big House," no one ever saw Mr. Anderson again, even on the "Big Road." This catastrophic event was the topic of conversation for many months to come in the cafes and on the street corners. The locals still made trips down the lane to take a look at the "Big House," and every once in a while, someone would say he or she saw Mr. Anderson, but that rumor was never substantiated. Or, sometimes someone was positive they saw activity around the house, but there never was any evidence of it. It was not long before there were no longer lights in the windows; the weeds overtook the flowers; the bushes went untrimmed and the grass was not mowed. No cars were ever seen traveling the gravel road down to the "Big House" unless it was one of the local residents doing a little snooping.

Chapter 5

A HOUSE DESERTED

The "Big House" remained empty for several years and began to have an unkempt, run down appearance. Weeds grew tall where there were once beautiful flowers; the bushes grew scraggly and no longer held their exquisite shapes; rotting leaves piled high in the corners of the fence; a gutter hung precariously on one side of the house swaying in the wind and rain; the front door looked as though it needed a coat of paint and fruit lay rotting on the ground. The frame of the swing set that had never had a child sit in one of the swings began to rust. Looking at the swings sitting silent in the sunshine would bring tears to the eyes of even the most hard-hearted person. No longer did the "Big House" elicit a sense of awe as it had when it was occupied by the Andersons.

Those first time visitors who came from surrounding communities to visit the pumpkin patch could see the magnificent structure set off in the distance and were curious about it. The questions were endless. Why was everything so run down? Why was the house empty? Where were the owners? Why did he leave such a beautiful house? What happened to the owners? Were there children living in it? What was going to happen to it? There were no answers to their questions.

Throughout the years, as the story about the building of the "Big House," the death of Mrs. Anderson and her unborn children and the disappearance of Mr. Anderson were repeated over and over, it took on a life of its own. One story was that Mr. Anderson was so distraught after the death of his wife and his stillborn children that he threw himself in the river, and his body was never found. Another story was that he was so depressed he went berserk and had to be institutionalized. A new story of what happened to him would surface every once in a while. Of course, there was no factual basis to any of the stories. They only popped up when someone let their imagination run wild. It got to the point where even the locals were beginning to wonder what part of the stories were real and what had been made up.

  As the "Big House" stood desolately on the grounds with weeds growing taller and taller, rotted leaves piling up higher and higher around the fence and the bushes growing over the windows, the residents of Calvary spent many hours wondering and discussing what was going to happen to it. The stately house looked so sad sitting against the horizon.

  Was it going to be torn down? Would someone buy it and fix it up to live in? Would it remain empty forever? What else could be done with it? No one had any answers about what was going to happen, but it gave the locals something to talk about. When all was calm in Calvary and there were few topics of discussion, the conversation would turn to the "Big House." One thing the residents of Calvary knew was that there was no one in their little town wealthy enough to buy the property, much less repair it.

Chapter 6

THE "BIG HOUSE" RE-BORN

Eventually discussions about the "Big House" began to wane. Then one sunny day, trucks of all sizes were spotted turning off the highway heading down the gravel lane toward the "Big House." Wow, this was big news, and it did not take long for it to spread through the neighborhoods! In Calvary, all it took was for one person to hear or see something, and before long, the whole town would know. Gossip traveled fast in that little community!

The activity around the "Big House" caused a lot of excitement and speculation about what was happening. Whenever there were a few people gathered together, it was not long before the topic was inserted into the conversation. For several weeks, they watched the flurry of activity up and down the lane. None of the workmen ever came into Calvary so there was no way they could be questioned. The wrought iron gate in front of the property remained closed and locked so no one from Calvary could get in, although a couple of people tried. All they could do was watch the activity from afar.

The weeds were cut down, leaves and sticks were raked up, bushes were once again trimmed into beautiful shapes, trees were pruned, gutters were fixed, window casings were painted, the front door was painted a bright red, the creaky swing set was removed and a new one was set up. Once the weeds were under control, a few flowers could even be seen swaying in the breeze. The "Big House"

THE "BIG HOUSE" RE-BORN

was being brought back to its original, stately splendor. It once again looked like a "happy house."

The new swing set really caused a lot of speculation. Questions, questions! Was there a family moving in with children? What else could it be? Who was rich enough to buy the property? Where were they coming from? Was Mr. Anderson coming back? Had he remarried and planned on having a family? No one had any answers, but that did not stop anyone from asking the questions, not really expecting an answer. Work on the "Big House" brought an air of excitement and expectation to Calvary.

After several months of whirlwind activity, there were fewer large work trucks going up and down the lane. A few cars and a truck were seen headed down the lane to the "Big House," but these did not leave. They would remain for several days. Lights began to twinkle in the windows at night so the town folk knew that once again, someone was living in the "Big House." Occasionally a worker could be seen in the yard or someone would be walking around on the porch. Everyone in Calvary was very curious and pondered about what was happening, even though they had nothing to base any of their ideas on.

Of course, there were always a few in Calvary whose curiosity got the best of them. They drove down the gravel lane on several occasions to see if there was a clue as to who was occupying the "Big House." They never came back with any more information than what they had when they began their treks, but that did not keep them from playing detective.

Chapter 7

A NEW BEGINNING FOR THE "BIG HOUSE"

The town busybody, Samantha Davis, could not resist driving out quite often. Early one morning just as the sun was coming up, she decided to make another trip down the lane to the "Big House" to try to see what was going on. To her surprise, as she drove down the lane, in the front yard she saw a large white sign with red lettering hanging inside the big wrought iron gate that said "Anderson Calvary Orphanage." She was so excited she could hardly get her car turned around fast enough. She drove as fast as she could to get to the Corner Cafe to tell the news to all those who would listen, and she was certain that everyone would listen! This was big news!

Between being out of breath from running into the Cafe and being excited about what she saw, Samantha could hardly tell her story. Everyone kept asking her questions, but all she could tell them was that she saw the sign that said "Anderson Calvary Orphanage." They teased her that maybe she just had a dream. Samantha got in a snit and told them to drive out and take a look. They finally quit teasing her and decided that she must have seen the sign and was telling the truth.

After hearing Samantha's story, no one lingered after they had their breakfast that morning. They all wanted to be among the first to spread the news in their neighborhood. It was not long before the telephone line was buzzing, and people were chatting on the street corners, or over the

A NEW BEGINNING FOR THE "BIG HOUSE"

backyard fence. All of the activity around the "Big House" had caused a tremendous amount of excitement in Calvary, but this was even more exciting because now they knew what the "Big House" was going to be used for. It was the main topic of conversation for several days no matter where you were – in the cafes, in the grocery store, the hardware store, the doctor's office. There was no other topic of conversation! An orphanage in Calvary – why in their little town? Where were the children going to come from? Who had the money to fix up the "Big House?" Who owned the orphanage? Who was going to run the orphanage?

The "Big House" had always elicited a lot of curiosity and questions. Now there was just a different set of questions, and they still did not have any answers to this new set of questions.

As the story was told, Busybody Samantha made a few more trips down the gravel road to see what she could find out. She was bound and determined that she was going to find out the whole story behind this orphanage. One day, she saw a man raking leaves around the wrought iron fence. Without hesitation, she marched right up to the fence to talk to him. After introducing herself and trying to wheedle some answers out of him, she finally decided that he had told her all he knew, or at least all he was going to divulge to her, when he went back to his raking.

The yardman told Samantha that he was just an employee and did not know much about the circumstances surrounding the "Big House." He had heard that there was a wealthy man named Anderson who had lived in this house at one time. He wanted it turned into an orphanage because he had lived in an orphanage as a child. That was all the information he could give her.

It was not much, but at least it was a little tidbit of gossip that Samantha could take back to the customers of the Corner Café. It was not gossip to Samantha, it was just "news." She delighted in knowing something that no one else did, but she could never keep it a secret. Samantha hurried back to town as fast as she could to spread the word. She was quite proud of herself for being the first to see the sign, Anderson Calvary Orphanage, and now she had even more news! Samantha did not consider herself a gossip or a busybody. According to her, she was doing her duty as a resident of Calvary by keeping her eyes and ears open. Not all of the locals agreed with Samantha, but basically she was harmless!

Samantha, along with the rest of the town folk, kept a close eye on the orphanage for the next few weeks to see what else would develop. Every day, somebody would drive down the lane to the orphanage gates just to see if they could find out something, but usually had nothing to report. No one ever knew where the children came from, but one by one, they did come. Occasionally, cars that were unfamiliar to anyone in the community would be seen driving down the lane toward the orphanage and would be let into the big, wrought iron gate. When this happened it was big news in Calvary!

It was not long before several children of all ages could be seen running around the yard playing games and playing on the swing set. There were always one or two adults outside with the children. Small groups of children could even be seen taking trips over the footbridge that spanned

A NEW BEGINNING FOR THE "BIG HOUSE"

the Calvary River. On the other side of the footbridge was a small sandy beach, another swing set, a bench and a forest of trees as a backdrop.

Chapter 8

CALVARY PUMPKIN PATCH

It did not take long for Anderson Calvary Orphanage to become an integral part of the community, even though the local residents saw little of the children or the staff members. The residents quickly adopted them as part of their community. The townsfolk were so proud of "their orphanage," you would have thought that they had in some way been responsible for it being in their community.

As the months and years went by, the orphanage did not garner as much attention from the Calvary residents as it once did, nor was it the topic of conversation all of the time, but it did attract the attention of those that were new to the area. Visitors always had questions about how an orphanage came to be in existence next to a pumpkin patch in a small town like Calvary. When the questions were asked, the answers might not always be the same. Throughout the years of re-telling the story of the "Big House" and the Andersons, it took a few twists and turns, and was rarely repeated the same way twice. Regardless of how the questions were answered, you could tell that everyone in Calvary was proud of the Anderson Calvary Orphanage and the Calvary Pumpkin Patch. They loved to tell stories about the orphanage and the pumpkin patch, and everyone was sure that the story they told was the correct one.

The children that lived in the orphanage were not seen in town on a regular basis, but they did make visits to the pumpkin patch from the time the first little green vine pushed its way through the earth until the last pumpkin was harvested. The children particularly liked to go when the pumpkins were ready to be picked, and they were allowed to pick out their own Jack-O-Lantern. They ran through the patch squealing with delight as they scampered from one pumpkin to another. The little tykes could be seen sitting on the larger pumpkins, and sometimes tumbling off, which made all of the volunteers smile. The volunteers working in the patch always welcomed the children and made a special effort to make sure each one picked out just the perfect pumpkin.

    The volunteers that worked at the pumpkin patch on a regular basis had the opportunity to get to know the children during their visits. Each year they would notice that a few they had gotten to know did not return, and there would be children they had not seen before. They would assume that those who did not return had been adopted. The children were always accompanied by workers from the orphanage, but they never divulged any information to the volunteers about the children.

    It was a mystery as to where the families came from to adopt the children and how they knew about the orphanage. The only clue was that cars with license plates from various states would be seen coming to or leaving the orphanage. It was assumed that they were people looking to adopt one or more of the children. Evidently the reputation of the orphanage for having happy, well-adjusted children had spread far and wide.

    A few of the children who were never adopted spent

Jenny's Angel

their young lives at the orphanage so they became well known to the pumpkin patch volunteers, and the children became well acquainted with the volunteers. Throughout the years, with all of the visits the children made to the pumpkin patch, a special bond developed between the volunteers and the children. The volunteers never had anything but praise for the children and the staff members that accompanied the children to the pumpkin patch. They were delightful, well behaved, happy children. The volunteers could see the love that the staff members had for the children and the children had for the staff members. They were all one big, happy family. After every visit, the volunteers would take stories back to the townsfolk about what a special place the orphanage must be to have such happy children.

Chapter 9

MIRACLE IN A BASKET

    One cold, November night, Jake was making one last trip to the front gate to make sure it was locked. Keeping the orphanage safe and secure was one of his most important duties, and he took it very seriously. He had already been out once to check the lock on the gate just a short time earlier, but wanted to have peace of mind when he quit for the evening. He was headed out to check it one last time. There had been a great deal of activity at the orphanage that day, with several people coming and going. The staff was getting ready for the Thanksgiving holiday so a lot of deliveries had been made.

    Every staff member always put forth an extra effort to make all holidays special for the children. Although most of the children had never experienced living in a family setting and celebrating holidays, they all had the feeling that they were special because the staff members made them feel that way. Most of the staff members lived at the orphanage so they all felt like one big family. Once a person became a staff member at the orphanage, he or she rarely left their employment. There was just something very special about the Anderson Calvary Orphanage.

Jake was one of the staff members that lived on the premises. He had a small cabin at the rear of the property that had originally been built for the caretaker of the "Big House." Jake was far more than just a night watchman, even though that is what he had been hired as. He had been at the orphanage since it first opened and did whatever was necessary. He kept the premises secure, worked in the garden, did repairs, ran errands and any other task that Mrs. Miller asked him to do. Sometimes he even had to make a quick trip into town to the grocery store. He loved living at the orphanage, but most of all, he loved the children, and they loved him. Some of the children even called him Grampa Jake, which thrilled him. He had never married and, therefore, had no children, so this was his family. Jake did not feel like he was "working" at the orphanage – he was just taking care of his family!

The air was sharp and the dry leaves crunched under his feet as Jake walked down the path in the yard to the front gate. Most of the leaves had fallen from the large oak trees that surrounded the grounds. The few leaves that were still hanging on the limbs rustled as the wind blew through the bare branches making an eerie, lonely sound. Jake shivered and buttoned up his coat as he hastened his pace. If it got much colder, he was going to have to put his light jacket away and dig his winter coat out of the closet.

It had been a long day, and Jake was tired. He was ready to get back to his cabin, kick off his work boots and prop up his feet. As he scurried toward the big iron gate, he looked around the grounds making sure that nothing appeared to be out of place. He always carried his big lantern when he went out at night to flash around the yard as he walked. If the sky was full of clouds, and there was no moonlight, the grounds were quite dark once he got away from the house. The windows were covered with curtains which did not allow for much light to escape. Jake was sure he could walk the grounds of the orphanage blindfolded

MIRACLE IN A BASKET

since he spent so much time outside, but he never knew if a toy had been left outside on the path, so he always carried his lantern.

When Jake got to the gate, he reached up to make sure the lock was secure, and he was happy to see that it was. He flashed his lantern around and everything appeared to be as it should be. No toys were lying around, the gate was locked, and he was ready to quit. As he turned, he muttered to himself, "I am done for the day, and I am ready for a rest."

Jake had taken only a few steps back up the path toward the house when he thought he heard the tinkling sound of a bell. He stopped and looked back for a few seconds to listen. All was quiet. He turned back and took a few more steps up the path, but there was that tinkling sound again. No, he must be imagining that he was hearing a bell. The church was too far away to hear its bells ringing. Maybe the wind was blowing in the right direction and carrying the sound in his direction. That did not make any sense because it was too late for the church bells to be ringing. He started up the path again, and there was that tinkling sound again. This time he knew he had to turn around and investigate where that sound was coming from, or he would not rest easy in his cabin.

Jake was chilled to the bone, but he had to satisfy his curiosity and find out where that sound was coming from. The leaves on the trees could not be making that tinkling sound. Maybe a toy was left outside that had a bell on it, and he had not seen it He pointed his lantern all around the yard once again, but did not see anything. Jake turned and slowly walked the few steps back to the big, wrought

Jenny's Angel

iron gate. He looked around very slowly into the distance and shined the lantern into the darkness, but could not see anything out of the ordinary. He was convinced there was something amiss, but what was it? He was not afraid, but was beginning to be a little uneasy.

Jake turned his lantern downward checking the ground around the base of the brick pillar where one end of the gate was fastened. He slowly walked the length of the gate and kept his lantern shining on the ground. He heard the tinkling sound again. Was the wind playing tricks on his ears? There was another brick post at the other end where the wrought iron gate was connected and latched. He had just checked the large chain and padlock on the gate. It was much too heavy to be blown around by the wind. As he got closer to the post, he thought he saw something on the ground outside the gate. He shined the lantern toward the object and was stunned to see a large basket sitting on the ground by the brick pillar. That must be where the tinkling sound was coming from. He squatted down to see if he could see anything in the basket. As the lantern light was reflected on the basket, he could see a bell tied to the top of the basket handle. That sent cold chills down his spine, and it was not from the cold air. At least he had found the source of the tinkling sound but his mind was whirling.

Why was a basket sitting by the gate? Jake stood up quickly and looked around, shining his lantern in all directions. He could not see anyone, or anything that was unusual. How did that basket get there? How long had it been there? What was in it? Questions raced through his mind.

MIRACLE IN A BASKET

Jake knew he had to open the gate and see what was in the basket, although he was reluctant to do so. He hurriedly turned his lantern off and set it on the ground. He did not know whether he should open the gate by himself, or run back to the orphanage and get someone else. All kinds of thoughts flew through his mind. Could someone be lurking around just waiting for him to open the gate? Was someone trying to get into the orphanage? Maybe someone was playing a prank!

Jake decided he would take a chance that no one was going to jump out of the bushes. He would unlock the padlock, open the gate, grab the basket and lock the padlock as quickly as possible. His lantern was a big one so if he had to use it as a club, he would. Jake was never afraid on the orphanage grounds, even on the darkest night, but this was really strange and made him very nervous. Someone had placed that basket there not too long before because he had made his usual rounds of the grounds about 30 minutes earlier. He did not know if there was anything in that basket, but he had to check it out, or he would never get any sleep tonight. He was glad he had decided to check the gate one more time.

Jake took the lock off, opened the gate and grabbed the basket as quickly as he could. Without even looking in the basket, he set it on the ground and quickly wrapped the chain around the wrought iron fence and hurriedly slipped the padlock on. He did not know if someone was lurking around, but he was not taking any chances by tarrying.

Jake grabbed the basket and his lantern and hurried up the path to the house. The basket was made of wicker and

Jenny's Angel

was not very heavy. Jake was very curious as to what was inside, but he still did not stop to take a peak. Maybe there was nothing of importance inside. Maybe someone had set it there earlier that day as they left the orphanage and forgot to take it with them. But, no, this could not be because he had been to the gate earlier, and he was positive that he had not seen the basket nor had he heard the tinkling of the bell. Someone had set that basket there just in the past 30 minutes. It was a puzzlement!

Jake ran as fast as he could while holding the basket and his lantern, and the little bell tinkled all the way. He was tired and cold and just wanted to get into the warmth of the house. Lights could be seen in several of the windows so he knew that some of the resident staff members had not yet gone to bed, even though all of the children would be tucked away and sound asleep. Mrs. Miller was always the last one to go to her room after everyone else was settled in, and she made sure all the lights were turned off except for a couple of small lamps.

As Jake barged through the front door, a welcoming blast of warm air rushed out. He quickly shut the door and hurried to the chair closest to the fireplace. The glowing embers from which a little heat emanated were a welcome sight. He set the basket down on the floor in front of him. He was anxious to see what was inside, but was almost afraid to look. How silly, he thought. Maybe someone had just left a basket of fruit or vegetables. He quite often found items left at the gate during the daylight hours, but no one had ever left anything at night.

A soft, white flannel blanket was tucked loosely

MIRACLE IN A BASKET

all around the edges. Why would anyone cover fruit or vegetables with a blanket? He could not imagine what was in this basket! Maybe he should find Mrs. Miller first. No, he was sure there was nothing in the basket that was of very much importance, or it would not have been left by the gate on such a cold night.

Jake's fingers were cold and numb. He blew on them and rubbed them together to warm them up. He leaned over and gingerly tugged at one corner of the blanket. As he lifted the blanket, he heard a faint sound that almost sounded like a cat. Had someone left a basket full of kittens? His mind was spinning. He stopped and his hands were shaking. He gave the blanket another tug and pulled it half way back. He was so shocked at what he saw that all he could do was sit and stare for a few seconds. He could not believe what he was looking at. There nestled in the bottom of the basket was a baby. No, his eyes must be playing tricks on him. It must be a life sized doll. No, it was a baby! He was so befuddled he could not think straight. Was the baby alive? It was! He saw the little pink fingers on one hand move.

Jake jumped up and started hollering for Mrs. Miller. He had never been so confused in all his life. He was making such a racket it did not take Mrs. Miller long to hurry out of the kitchen.

"What is all of this yelling about, Jake? Are you hurt? Calm down, or you will wake the children."

Jake was so excited he ran to Mrs. Miller, grabbed her arm and started pulling her over toward the fireplace. He was speechless and just pointed to the basket. Mrs. Miller spied the basket on the floor and quickly moved toward it. As she peered into the basket she was as shocked as Jake was. All they could do was stare down into the basket and then stare at each other. Now, she too was speechless.

Mrs. Miller picked up the basket and set it on a nearby table to get a better look. There lay a precious little baby sound asleep with its golden eyelashes resting on chubby pink cheeks. Jake had only pulled the blanket back far enough to uncover the baby's head and one little hand that rested on its cheek. Jake's trip up the path to the house and all of his yelling had not disturbed the baby which was certainly surprising. Mrs. Miller had taken care of a lot of babies, and she knew that this one looked like it was only a few weeks old.

Finally, Mrs. Miller was able to gather her thoughts and say something, although she was still astounded at seeing the baby. She looked at Jake and said, "Where did you get this basket?"

Jake's words tumbled out of his mouth so rapidly that Mrs. Miller could hardly understand what he was saying. She put her hand up to make him stop talking. Jake took a deep breath and tried to tell the story more slowly. Finally Mrs. Miller was able to understand enough about what Jake said to figure out that he had found the basket by the front gate. This was all the information she needed right now. She would get the whole story later when Jake was a little calmer. As she listened, she stared first at Jake, and then down at the baby. She was as baffled as he was.

MIRACLE IN A BASKET

Mrs. Miller touched the tiny hand, which felt warm and rubbed a tiny little cheek, which felt like a rose petal. Evidently the basket had not been sitting out in the cold very long because the baby was warm. Its head was covered in a knit cap pulled down over its ears. After piecing together the disjointed story Jake had told her, her only thought was that someone had been waiting on the gravel road to see if Jake would come down to check the gate, as he so often did. When they saw his lantern in the distance, someone must have crept quietly to the gate and set the basket down so he would see it. What a miracle that he found this precious little baby!

The longer they stood looking at the baby, the more they grinned at one another. Mrs. Miller told Jake to see if there were any other staff members in the kitchen, or in any of the other rooms, that had not retired for the night. They needed to get the baby out of the basket and see if they had a boy or a girl. Mrs. Miller was always very calm, but she was getting more excited by the minute. They had never had such a tiny baby at the orphanage. She knew that everyone would be as excited as she was.

Jake scurried off to see if he could find anyone. He was so excited that he was talking loudly and about the only word anyone could understand was "baby" and "come." There were a few people in the kitchen, and it did not take long for several others who were in their rooms to begin sticking their heads out of their doors wanting to know what was going on. No one knew for sure what was happening, but as excited as Jake was, it must be important. They did not want to miss out on whatever it was.

Jenny's Angel

Everyone always got excited whenever a new child arrived to be cared for, but the word "baby" got everyone's attention. Every child who came to live at the Anderson Calvary Orphanage was a very fortunate child, regardless of what the circumstances were. All of the staff members were devoted to taking care of the children and thought of it as their mission in life. They considered these children gifts from heaven. Sometimes the funds were a little tight, but the children never felt the strain of it.

It did not take long before most of the staff was standing around the table looking at the basket. Someone said, "We need to see if we have a boy or a girl." Mrs. Miller had a big smile on her face and nodded as she looked at Jake.

"Jake would you like to take the blanket off?"

With his hands shaking, he gently pulled the blanket back so they could see the rest of the baby. As he did this, everyone crowded around so they could see and immediately whispered, "It's a girl!" The baby was dressed in a ruffled pink crocheted dress with delicate, tiny, white bows. The dress was so long that it covered her legs. Jake lifted the hem of the dress. A little pink blanket was wrapped around her legs. Jake gently pulled this blanket back and white knitted booties peaked out. With his large calloused hands, he gently lifted her head and pulled her knitted cap off. Whoever had put this basket at the gate had dressed her with care so she would stay warm.

Jake looked up with tears in his eyes and with a catch in his voice said, "The baby has on pink. We must

MIRACLE IN A BASKET

have a girl."

By this time, everyone had tears in their eyes – happy tears—and big smiles on their faces. About that time, the little face in the basket scrunched up and let out a whimper which quickly turned into a wail so loud that it startled Jake. He had not been around tiny babies much so he had no idea what to do and looked up at Mrs. Miller. Mrs. Miller quickly lifted the little bundle out of the basket and started giving orders.

"Someone, see if you can find some diapers and baby powder. Somebody else needs to go to the pantry and find some milk and a bottle. Then see if you can find a cradle. This little lady might need a change and from the sound of her, she just might be hungry."

Everyone scurried off to see what they could find, but Jake stuck real close to Mrs. Miller. He was in awe of the child being cradled in Mrs. Miller's arms. She was absolutely beautiful even if she was crying, and her face was all scrunched up and red. Little tears squeezed out of her eyes and rolled down the sides of her tiny face into her ears. Jake was distraught at the sound of the wails.

It did not take long before a warm bottle of milk was handed to Mrs. Miller. She looked at Jake to see if he wanted to give it to the baby, but Jake shook his head "no." This one was too little for Jake to be comfortable with. Within seconds, the baby was sucking on the bottle and the tears had disappeared.

Within minutes, the baby's eyes began to drift shut

Jenny's Angel

again. A wooden cradle with a pad and blankets had been placed close to the fireplace. Mrs. Miller gently laid the little girl in it and covered her up with the blanket. Everyone crowded around to watch the sleeping child. They were all mesmerized.

Jake stood by the cradle as close as he could get. He could not take his eyes off that little bundle in the cradle. All of a sudden, the baby's eyes flew open. It looked like she was gazing straight at Jake with her large sparkling blue eyes. Their eyes locked, and she raised her little fists in the air. Jake reached down and put his finger on the baby's hand. The second he did, her little fingers curled around Jake's finger. It was almost as if she knew that Jake had rescued her, and he was her hero! Jake was speechless!

Everyone was peeping into the cradle and chattering softly at the same time. "What are we going to call her? Where do you think she came from? How old do you think she is? Will someone come for her and want her back?"

Chapter 10

JENNY

Of course, there were no answers to the questions, except they all were in agreement that she must be given a name. Mrs. Miller looked at Jake, then around at every one else and said, "Would anyone object to letting Jake pick out a name for this little one since he found her at the gate?"

Everyone murmured and nodded in agreement that this was a wonderful idea. Jake stood and stared, first at the baby then at Mrs. Miller and back at the baby. He was most generally a man of few words, but now he was absolutely speechless. You could have heard a pin drop in the room as they waited patiently for him to say something.

Names were flying through Jake's mind – Jane, Sally, Ellen, Judy, Linda, Mary, Christy, Addie. No, those names were not right. It had to be just the right name. All of a sudden, Jake's face broke into a wide grin. "Jenny, that's it. She looks like a Jenny. We will name her Jenny." Hesitantly, he looked around, and he asked, "Is that OK with everyone else?"

Everyone let out a sigh and several giggled. With smiles on their faces, they shook their heads in agreement that Jenny was what her name should be. Jake squatted by the cradle and said, "Little one, we don't know where you came from or what you have been called, but your name is now Jenny. You are our little blessing."

Jenny's Angel

Watching Jake peering into the cradle and talking to little Jenny brought a tear to everyone's eye. As the excitement of the evening started to dissipate, several of the staff members shuffled off to their rooms. A few of them stayed around chatting about the events of the evening and speculating about where Jenny came from. There were lots of exciting days at the orphanage, but not like this one!

Even though Jenny was sleeping soundly with a slight smile on her face, Mrs. Miller was sure that Jenny's diaper needed to be changed. She pulled the blanket back and took off the knitted booties. As she did that, she and Jake both let out a little gasp. A few others who had not left the room and were standing close enough to see Jenny's little legs and feet also let out a gasp. Jenny's right foot was turned in toward her other leg at a very unusual angle. Her little toes which should have been straight up were almost touching the side of her left leg. No one said anything, but just looked at each other. Something was wrong with that little foot.

Even though Jake was a man of few words, he broke the silence and spoke firmly as he looked at the sleeping child and then at those who were standing around. In a very serious tone he said, "Jenny is a precious little baby girl that was delivered to us tonight. Whoever left her at the gate knew that this orphanage is a special place and that we will take good care of her. Jenny is going to grow up to be a special little girl. We will love Jenny just as much as we love all of the other children."

No one had ever heard Jake say that many serious words at one time. Mrs. Miller looked around at everyone in the room and said adamantly, "I agree with Jake, and I am sure that everyone at this orphanage feels the same way. We have other children who have problems. We do not love them any less."

That broke the tension in the room and a smile broke out on everyone's face. They were all in agreement. At the orphanage, a deformity of any kind did not make the child any less important. Jenny would be loved! Everyone started chatting with each other.

It was always exciting when a child came to reside at the orphanage, but one had never been found in a basket! They all agreed that when the rest of the staff came to work the next day, and the children gathered for breakfast, they would be in for a big surprise. The story of how Jenny was found would be told over again and again.

Mrs. Miller finally got the diaper changed, and Jenny never made a peep. Those who were left in the room had to take one more peak at their new little resident before they went back to their rooms. Jake was distraught about Jenny's foot and wondered how she was going to learn to walk. Mrs. Miller could see the concern on Jake's face. His brow was furrowed, and he was pacing the floor. Mrs. Miller assured Jake that they would do all they could to help Jenny. Jake did not want to leave and wanted to know who was going to take care of Jenny. He would like to have taken her to his cabin, but he knew he could not do that. He did not know anything about changing diapers and fixing bottles!

Mrs. Miller convinced Jake that she personally would take care of Jenny, and he could go to his cabin.

Jenny's Angel

Before he left, Mrs. Miller had Jake carry the cradle to her bedroom. Once again, Jenny never made a peep. With her diaper changed and tummy full, she was sound asleep. Reluctantly Jake left, but told Mrs. Miller that he would be back early the next morning to check on Jenny and help her with the cradle. Mrs. Miller stifled a little chuckle as Jake left the room. He certainly was smitten by this little one.

Mrs. Miller stood and gazed out of her bedroom window. She saw the wind whipping the bare tree limbs to and fro. It even looked like it was spitting snow. Little droplets of water appeared on the window pane where the tiny snowflakes landed. She shivered as the cold air radiated from the window pane. She was so thankful that Jake decided to check the front gate one more time. That was a miracle in itself. She shuddered as she thought about what would have happened to Jenny if he had not. Even though Jenny was wrapped snugly in blankets and had a little cap on, she would not have survived through the night in this cold weather. Questions rolled around in Mrs. Miller's mind. Who were Jenny's parents? Were they from Calvary or from another town in the area? Why did they just leave her at the gate instead of trying to make arrangements for her care? What were they going to do about her foot? She had no answers, but she knew that the staff would love and care for Jenny the same way they cared for all of the other children.

Mrs. Miller always met the challenges at the orphanage head on and this would be no different. Jenny was not the first child to come to the orphanage with some type of disability, or with little known about the child's background. The orphanage did not have a lot of

JENNY

extra money for special medical care or equipment, and sometimes they had a hard time finding the right type of equipment, but God always provided. Sometimes they would find a tiny wheel chair at their front gate or a tiny pair of crutches just at the time that they were needed. They rarely knew where the items came from, but put them to use and were thankful. She was confident that Jenny would somehow receive the care she needed.

Chapter 11

AN ANGEL ON EARTH – THE DOCTOR

Dr. Carlson was one of the doctors in Calvary, and he made visits to the orphanage twice a month to see the children. He had approached the orphanage as soon as it opened and offered his services. Mrs. Miller was overwhelmed with his offer – he would assume care of the children at no charge. She just could not believe what he said, but as the time passed and she never received a bill, she once again knew that she was on the receiving end of a miracle.

Sometimes there would be a sick one or two for Dr. Carlson to see, and other times he would just visit for a short while. He never seemed to tire of talking to them and trying to make them laugh. The children loved to see him come because many times he had a sucker for them. Dr. Carlson would even come at any time during the night, or on a weekend, if there was an emergency. He was a real blessing to the orphanage.

Mrs. Miller often marveled at the blessings that were continually bestowed upon the orphanage – equipment, Dr. Carlson's services, donations of clothing and the envelopes of money appearing just when it was needed most. All of these happenings just confirmed in her mind that Anderson Calvary Orphanage was a special place.

After feeding Jenny one more time and changing her diaper, Mrs. Miller decided that she would call Dr. Carlson in the morning and ask him to come and check Jenny over. She was sure Jenny was OK, but she just wanted to make sure. She would also talk to Dr. Carlson about Jenny's foot when he came to see her. Maybe that would help to relieve Jake's mind. She had never dealt with a deformed foot like Jenny's and was anxious to hear whether Dr. Carlson had any suggestions.

When morning came, and the staff and the children found out about Jenny, there was a lot of excitement and commotion. It did not take long for everyone in the dining hall at breakfast to know that Mrs. Miller had a baby in her room that Jake had found by the gate in a basket. Everybody wanted to see the baby. Mrs. Miller chuckled at how excited everyone was. She had not left her room, but they were making so much noise she could hear the chatter. Several of the older children that had been there since they were small had seen many children come to the orphanage, but Jenny was different. Jenny had been found in a basket!

After giving Jenny a bottle and changing her diaper, Mrs. Miller wrapped her in her blanket and took her to the dining hall so the staff and children could take a peek at her. The level of the chatter got even louder as she started to enter the dining hall. Most of the children came running and tried to crowd around her. She was afraid that all of the noise was going to wake Jenny so she handed her to one of the staff and motioned for her to leave the dining hall with Jenny. Then all she heard were groans from the children.

Mrs. Miller had to get the children calmed down and into their seats at their tables. She had never seen them so excited. Once everyone was in their seats, she brought the

Jenny's Angel

baby into the room and walked around at each of the tables so the children could see Jenny. Their eyes got big when they saw how tiny she was. They were full of questions, and some of them wanted to touch her tiny fingers or rub her head. Mrs. Miller patiently answered their questions, if she had the answers. Finally, she told the children to eat their breakfast because Jenny was going to be staying with them. They would get to see her all the time.

Mrs. Miller had changed her mind about asking Dr. Carlson to come to the orphanage. She decided that she and Jake would take Jenny into his office after lunch to have her checked out and to talk about Jenny's foot. Jake was elated that Mrs. Miller asked him to go to Dr. Carlson's office. He could hardly wait to get finished with his morning chores and to have lunch. The time seemed to drag by.

About 2:00 p. m., Mrs. Miller found Jake in the storeroom where he was building some extra shelves and told him that it was time to go. He gladly put his tools away and washed his hands. Maybe he would get a chance to have Jenny take hold of one of his fingers again so he wanted to make sure they were clean. Jenny was back in her basket and seemed to be very comfortable so that is how she took her first ride in to Calvary.

The trip into town did not take long and soon the three of them were sitting in Dr. Carlson's examining room. They were fortunate that Dr. Carlson was not extremely busy that afternoon and was able to see them. Mrs. Miller was quite anxious to have Jenny checked out even though she knew Jenny was OK. She was very protective of all the children in the orphanage. To her, they were God's special, little children that had been entrusted to be cared for at the orphanage, and she was going to do her very best to take care of them.

They did not have to wait long for Dr. Carlson to come into the room. He looked at the bundle in the basket and said, "Well, what do you have here? It looks like you have someone new for me to see."

Jake jumped right in and told Dr. Carlson about finding the basket by the gate with the baby in it. Mrs. Miller was amused at Jake's eagerness to tell Dr. Carlson how he had found Jenny. Jake was usually not very talkative, but that was certainly not true where Jenny was concerned. Dr. Carlson frowned and thought for a few minutes without speaking. Before he could say anything, Jake's face got red and he hurriedly said, "We don't know who left her, but we want to keep her. We have named her Jenny and she is going to be our baby."

"OK, OK, Jake. I am not going to try to take Jenny away from the orphanage. I was just trying to think if I knew of anyone who had given birth to a child in the past few weeks. I cannot think of anyone, so it must be someone from out of the area that knows about the orphanage. It was fortunate for this little gal that you found her when you did. She probably would not have survived the night with the cold weather we are having."

Jake let out a sigh of relief! Mrs. Miller told Dr. Carlson that she was sure Jenny was just fine, but wanted him to check her out. Dr. Carlson asked Mrs. Miller a lot of questions as he examined Jenny. How was she eating?

Jenny's Angel

Did she have any trouble with the bottle? How were her diapers? Was she sleeping? Was she fussy?

When he finished examining Jenny, he said, "This little gal seems to be in good health. I know that you both have seen Jenny's little foot that is turned in. This is going to make it difficult for her to learn to walk."

Jake immediately chimed in, "We know she is not perfect, but that's OK. She's perfect to us, and we will help her learn to walk."

Dr. Carlson looked at Jake with a smile and said, "Jake, it looks like this little one has already captured your heart."

Jake's cheeks turned a bright red as he glanced over at Mrs. Miller.

"That's OK, Jake. She is a beautiful little girl, and I know that she will get along just fine. She is not going to be walking for many months. I would suggest that several times each day, you have someone massage her little foot and gently put some pressure on the ankle to try to turn it back so that her toes are pointing upward instead of toward her other leg. In time, it might help her bones to move a little in that direction. Work her ankle gently around in a circle and that might help a little also. I would suggest you have just one person work with her so that what is being done will be consistent. I know that all of your staff members are caring people, but pick someone that particularly likes babies. I will check her foot each time I come to see the other children to see if any progress is being made. That is about all we can do at this time. If you want to take her to another doctor in the city, then you can do that. Other than that, I think Jenny is just fine."

He looked at Jake and said with a grin on his face, "And, I am sure that Jenny is going to get a lot of attention." Jake's cheeks turned red again, and he grinned from ear to ear.

Chapter 12

JENNY THRIVES

Little Jenny thrived with the care she received, as did all of the children at the orphanage. One of the younger staff members, a young lady by the name of Elizabeth, was assigned the task of massaging Jenny's foot and working her ankle three times each day. Jenny was such a delightful, happy baby that Miss Elizabeth was more than happy to take time out of her morning and afternoon duties with the other children to spend time with Jenny. The rest of the time Jenny spent in the nursery with the other babies.

Every time Jake walked by the nursery, he would pop his head in the door and ask about Jenny. The nursery workers, or Miss Elizabeth, gave him a progress report about every little thing that Jenny did – her first smile, her cooing, her first laugh and let him look at Jenny's foot. Jake loved hearing every little tidbit.

As the weeks and months went by, Jenny's foot began to respond to the massaging and her ankle was not as rigid as when Miss Elizabeth first started working with Jenny. It would never be normal, but every little bit of progress delighted everyone.

Jenny soon learned to recognize Jake and would squeal with delight when she saw him. It did not take long for a very special bond to develop between the two of them. Jake worried and fretted over Jenny's little foot and wondered how she was going to learn to walk and run. He

JENNY THRIVES

could see that some progress was being made, but he still worried about her.

All of Jake's worrying was done in vain. By the time Jenny was two years old, she was scurrying around the nursery from one toy to another on her twisted foot. Everyone knew when Jenny was near because of the thump-thump sound her foot made as it struck the wooden floor when she was in a big hurry, and Jenny was most always in a hurry! At other times, they could hear her dragging it on the floor.

When Jenny fell down, and Jake was watching, you could see a pained look in his eyes. He wanted to rush over and help Jenny, but Mrs. Miller and Miss Elizabeth encouraged Jake to let Jenny learn to fall and get back up. Jake's sadness did not last long though, because Jenny never cried when she fell. She would let out one of her heartwarming squeals and delight everyone with her infectious laugh. Then Jake would relax and enjoy his time watching Jenny. How could anyone be sad when they heard Jenny's laugh?

Jenny had big round eyes as blue as the sky, long curls the color of a wheat field and did not have trouble keeping up with the other children of her age. She might look somewhat clumsy in her endeavors, but that never kept Jenny from trying to join in whatever activity was going on.

Even though several of the children in the orphanage were too young to attend the sessions in the school rooms, that did not mean they did not have a structured day, just as the school aged children did. They had play time each day,

Jenny's Angel

but they also had periods of time when they were taught skills like dressing themselves, tying their shoes, picking up their toys, learning the ABC's, and their numbers. Mrs. Miller felt that it was important for children to start learning at an early age. The younger children went to the dining hall with the older ones when it was meal time. When it came time for playtime in the yard though, they were kept separate from the older children. This was a matter of safety more than anything else.

Jenny had a sunny disposition and rarely was the least bit out of sorts. It did not matter whether she was trying to learn to tie the one shoe she wore, or running awkwardly around the yard, she was giggling or laughing at something. When Jenny was around she would bring a smile to everyone's face. Her happiness was contagious.

As Jenny grew through the toddler years, she recognized that she had a crippled foot. She never cried about it or acted as though she was different from the other children, nor did anyone treat her as though she was different. This was the philosophy that Mrs. Miller instilled in all of the staff.

Even though Jenny never complained about her foot, Jake could see that she would wince once in a while as she was running about. Sometimes she had trouble keeping up with the other children, but she never complained. It was particularly difficult for Jenny when the children went outside during the cold weather, or if it was wet. Jenny's twisted foot was was always padded and wrapped in a sock, but Jake just knew that there had to be a better solution. Mrs. Miller had put Jenny in a bedroom on the main floor

JENNY THRIVES

because going up and down the steps was one of the harder tasks that Jenny had to conquer.

Jake fretted and spent many hours thinking about what could be done. One day, he decided to ask Mrs. Miller if they could take Jenny to a shoe cobbler in the Big City to see if he could make a pair shoes that would fit Jenny's good foot and her crippled foot. Mrs. Miller was reluctant at first, but after listening to Jake plead with her, she finally consented to making the trip. She did not think that Jake would be satisfied until they checked it out.

Mrs. Miller told Jake that the orphanage did not have extra funds at that time so it would depend on what a pair of shoes for Jenny would cost. Jake told Mrs. Miller that he had been saving his money and would help pay for the shoes if necessary. He wanted Jenny to have two shoes so badly that if the orphanage could not pay for them, then he would buy them. He was determined that Jenny was going to have shoes just like all of the other little girls.

Mrs. Miller, Jake and Jenny headed for the Big City one warm fall day in October when it was getting close to Jenny's fifth birthday. No one knew what day Jenny was born on so they celebrated her birthday on November 1st each year. The car was warm with the sun shining through the windshield. The leaves on the trees were turning brilliant shades of red and gold. It was a perfect day for a drive into the Big City. Jake was apprehensive about what the results of their trip would be, but they had to try to get a shoe for Jenny's crippled foot.

Jenny had never been off the grounds of the

Jenny's Angel

orphanage except when Dr. Carlson had examined her a few days after she had been found in the basket at the gate. And, she certainly had no recollection of that. All three of them sat in the front seat, with Jenny tucked in between Jake and Mrs. Miller. She was mesmerized by what she saw as they sped along – a barn, a tractor, cows in the field, a couple of horses, a silo - things that she had only seen in a story book. She jabbered all of the way calling out the names of everything. When they arrived in the Big City, Jenny sat wide-eyed as she watched the cars zipping by and looked at the buildings. They did not have to worry about Jenny getting fidgety on the trip. She was spellbound by everything she saw.

Chapter 13

THE SHOE COBBLER

When they reached the cobbler's leather shop, Jake picked Jenny up out of the car and carried her, as she held tightly to his neck. Jenny was not a very big child so it was not a chore for Jake to carry her. As soon as Mrs. Miller opened the door, the smell of leather permeated the air. A bell on the top of the door tinkled, and the cobbler poked his head out from a back room. He was a big burly man with a bushy, red beard and a head of unruly hair. Mrs. Miller introduced herself and Jenny and Jake to the cobbler. Jenny's eyes were wide with apprehension as she clung to Jake's neck even tighter as she stared at the cobbler.

After explaining the situation about Jenny's foot and their purpose for coming to see him, the cobbler told Jake to sit Jenny on the counter. Jenny hung on tight to Jake's neck, but Jake assured her that it was OK. He told her that he would stay close. Jenny grabbed Jake's hand just to make sure that he did not go anywhere.

Jenny sat very quietly as the cobbler examined her foot for quite some time. For several minutes all he said was "Humm" over and over as he looked at one foot and then the other. This was making Jake very nervous. He could feel the beads of perspiration popping out on his forehead. Even Mrs. Miller was beginning to wonder if he was going to tell them that he could not make shoes for Jenny.

Finally, the cobbler smiled at Jenny and said, "Would

Jenny's Angel

you like to have a pair of shoes to wear, young lady?"

Jenny's eyes lit up like the stars in the sky on a dark night and said, "Oh, yes. I like to run and jump and play. Sometimes I get a sore on my foot, and it gets cold."

"Well," the cobbler said, "Young lady, this might be quite a challenge but I think I can fix you up. At least, I will certainly try."

Mrs. Miller was quite relieved, but rather nervous and said, "We really appreciate that you have taken time to look at Jenny's foot, but first I need to know what a pair of shoes will cost. As I told you, we are from the Anderson Calvary Orphanage, and our funds are rather limited."

The cobbler looked at Mrs. Miller, then at Jenny and back at Mrs. Miller with a furrowed brow. Jake was so nervous, he could feel his heart racing. He wanted Jenny to have a pair of shoes more than anything else in the world. Just as he started to say something, the cobbler raised his hand. Jake stopped before he got the first word out. Jenny's big blue eyes stared at the cobbler. Mrs. Miller held her breath. All three of them were like statues waiting for the cobbler to say something. The only sound was the clock ticking on the wall.

A wide grin broke out on the shoe cobbler's face as he looked at Jake and then Mrs. Miller. He touched Jenny's soft, little cheek and said, "Young lady, when is your birthday?"

Before anyone could say anything, the cobbler

THE SHOE COBBLER

said, "No, I do not need to know. I am going to give you a birthday present now – a new pair of shoes made just for you."

Mrs. Miller gasped when she heard what the cobbler said. Jake could not contain himself and let out a yell. With a big smile, Jenny clapped her hands and said, "My birthday is soon. I will have new shoes for my birthday?"

She reached out her little arms to give the cobbler a hug which brought an even bigger grin to his face. Mrs. Miller and Jake were so thrilled they could hardly say a word. Finally, Mrs. Miller regained her composure and thanked the cobbler. Jake shook the cobbler's hand so long he thought it was going to fall off.

The cobbler took several measurements of Jenny's feet while she was sitting and again as she stood up on the counter. They watched as he wrote all the information down and made several sketches. Finally he asked Mrs. Miller if they could make another trip in two weeks. He thought he could have the shoes made by then. Before she could even answer, Jake piped up and said they would be back in two weeks. Mrs. Miller just looked at Jake and smiled.

On the way back to the orphanage, Jenny was no longer interested in looking out of the car window at the pastures and houses. All she could talk about was the new pair of shoes she was going to get. Mrs. Miller and Jake were as excited as Jenny, but they said very little and let Jenny chatter.

Every day Jenny would ask Mrs. Miller if it was

Jenny's Angel

time to pick up her new shoes. Jake was just as anxious as Jenny, and finally the day arrived. Mrs. Miller, Jake and Jenny piled back into the car and headed back to the Big City to the shoe cobbler's shop. Jenny chattered and sang songs about getting a new pair of shoes. Jenny had a big imagination and quite often made up stories and songs as she played. It did not take long before Mrs. Miller and Jake knew the words and sang along with her. It was a happy ride into the Big City.

As soon as the bell above the door tinkled, the shoe cobbler popped his head out of the back room. When he saw who was coming in the door, he reached for a pair of shoes from the shelf in front of him. He had spent a lot of time on the shoes and was very proud of the fine leather workmanship. The shoes were made of soft brown leather with six little eyelets for the shoe laces. He wanted the leather to be soft so it would form around Jenny's little crippled foot, but also support her ankle and protect it. He was as anxious as everyone else to see if they were going to fit properly.

As soon as Mrs. Miller, Jake and Jenny entered the cobbler's shop, Jenny watched every move the cobbler made. She never took her eyes off the shoes in his hands as he came out from his workshop and walked toward them. When the cobbler put the shoes on the counter, Jenny's face broke into a wide grin.

"Are those my new shoes?"

"They certainly are, little miss. I would make a guess that you have been anxious to have them. Sit down

THE SHOE COBBLER

right here on the counter, and let's try them on," replied the cobbler.

Jake sat Jenny down on the counter. This time she did not cling to Jake's hand as she did on their first trip. She and the cobbler were good friends now. Mrs. Miller removed the padding that was on Jenny's crippled foot and the shoe that was on the other foot. She put on a new pair of socks. A new pair of shoes deserved a new pair of socks! It did not take the cobbler long to slip the shoe on Jenny's good foot. It fit perfectly. Now for the crippled foot. Everyone held their breath as the cobbler gently worked at putting it on her crippled foot.

After the cobbler had tied the laces on both shoes, Jenny looked up at him as though she did not know what was going to happen next. The cobbler looked at Jenny and said, "Well, little miss, are you ready to try your new shoes and see how they feel?"

Jenny reached down and gently touched both of the shoes. They were not sure she was going to say anything. Finally, she looked up with those big blue eyes and said, "Oh yes, Mr. Cobbler. They are so pretty and soft. I love my new shoes."

The cobbler picked Jenny up and gently stood her down on the floor. He was like a gentle giant with a little doll in his hands. Jenny just stood there, first looking at her new shoes and then up at Mrs. Miller, Jake and the cobbler and then back at her new shoes. She had never had a shoe on each one of her feet. Her crooked foot had always been wrapped and then covered with a sock, and the shoe felt

Jenny's Angel

different. She wiggled her feet a little but just stood still.

"Well, little miss, are you going to try to walk in those new shoes?" asked the cobbler.

Hesitantly, Jenny took a few steps, twirled around and immediately fell down. Before Jake could reach down to pick her up, she let out one of her delightful peals of laughter and said, "I love my new shoes. I will be able to run even faster and my foot won't get sore. I know my foot is crooked, but I have a shoe for each foot."

Everyone let out a sigh of relief and tears glistened in their eyes. Of course, Jenny's foot would always be crooked, but even at her young age, Jenny always seemed to be able to see the bright side of every situation.

Jenny got up and grabbed the cobbler around his legs and gave him a big hug. Mrs. Miller, Jake and the cobbler all let out a big laugh. Jenny spent several minutes walking around the front of the shop while the three of them stood watching. It was a happy day for everyone.

The cobbler picked Jenny up, sat her back down on the counter and explained to her that if her shoes started to hurt her feet, or if she got any sores on them, to let Mrs. Miller know. Jenny shook her head that she would, but told them that her new shoes would not hurt her feet. Mrs. Miller knew that Jenny would outgrow them in a year, but they would deal with that situation when the time came. For now, Jenny had a shoe for each one of her feet!

Mrs. Miller and Jake thanked the shoe cobbler

THE SHOE COBBLER

repeatedly for being so kind as to make Jenny a pair of shoes. He assured them that it was a very special day for him to see Jenny in her new shoes. He smiled as the three of them left his shop. Jenny's crooked little foot still made a thumping sound as she hopped along, but she was a happy little girl. As he waved good bye to them, he vowed that he would make her a new pair of shoes each year. No child should have a crippled foot and not have a shoe to put on it – at least, not as long as he was around!

Every year, at the end of October, just in time for November 1 when Jenny's birthday was celebrated, a new pair of shoes arrived. The package would be addressed to Mrs. Miller, but big block letters were written on the outside of the package – Jenny's Shoes. Mrs. Miller would keep the package until November 1, and then show it to Jenny. Jenny would be so excited she would twirl in circles. Mrs. Miller was astounded each year when the package arrived, and was even more astounded when she put the shoes on Jenny's feet and they fit. She never did figure out how the cobbler knew what size to make the shoes, but she did not even question it. She often wondered if Jake somehow measured Jenny's foot and got the information to the cobbler, but she never asked. If Jake was doing that, she did not want to spoil his little secret. She was so thankful for the blessing of new shoes for Jenny.

Putting Jenny's new shoes on each year was a special event so Mrs. Miller always let Jake do it, and every year, they had to repeat the story of how the three of them made a trip to the Big City when she was almost five years old to have the first pair made. Jenny never tired of hearing this story and usually had a few tidbits to add in. When Jake

Jenny's Angel

slipped the new shoes on Jenny's feet and they fit perfectly, Jenny would let out her delightful squeals that made everyone laugh.

Chapter 14

HALLOWEEN PUMPKINS

The staff at the orphanage made every holiday special for the children, and Halloween was no exception. Carving the pumpkins into Jack-O-Lanterns was a special event, and a tradition that was never broken. Although the children did not go into Calvary to "trick or treat", they celebrated in other ways.

The pumpkin patch was a very special place for the children from the time the vines bloomed until the pumpkins were all gone. The children became excited just as soon as the first little, green vine sprouted through the soft soil and started winding its way across the patch. Their excitement never waned until the pumpkins were picked and carved. They would visit the pumpkin patch to see the blooms and were captivated when they saw the tiny pumpkins begin to form. Each time they visited, they would be amazed at how much the pumpkins had grown and would run through the patch trying to find the biggest one.

The volunteers from the church who tended to the pumpkin patch were always delighted to see the children visit from the orphanage. It did not take long for them to learn the names of the children, and they always had a special candy treat for the children when they came. The children loved the outings to the pumpkin patch. The teachers used it as a learning experience by having the children write stories about the trip the next day. Everyone

Jenny's Angel

made their visits so much fun that the children were not even aware of how the teachers were using the trips as a learning experience.

When the pumpkins were ripe for harvesting, the children would be taken over in small groups so each one of them could pick out a pumpkin of their very own. Excitement ran high throughout the classrooms when it was announced that it was "pumpkin picking day."

It was understood that the orphanage never had to pay for any of the pumpkins the children picked out. Over the years, a special bond had developed between the orphanage and the church administrators and volunteers. Once again, Mrs. Miller was grateful for all that was bestowed upon the children at the orphanage.

On pumpkin picking day, Jake would take one of the wagons and haul the children to the pumpkin patch. Several staff members would be there to help the children pick out a pumpkin. When this was done, Jake would load them and their pumpkins back into the wagon and then drive back to the orphanage as they held their pumpkins. The wagon was not very big, so Jake spent all day making trips back and forth. No matter what task Jake was asked to do, he did it willingly. He was officially hired as the "night watchman," but it did not take long before he was involved in all kinds of activities. He was a very important part of the orphanage family.

So that there was no quibbling about how big a pumpkin could be picked out, Mrs. Miller set a rule that for a jack-o-lantern, the child had to be able to pick the

HALLOWEEN PUMPKINS

pumpkin up. The little children started out with the smaller pumpkins, but knew that each year as they became stronger, they would be able to get a bigger pumpkin. This rule made for a lot less fussing each year. Seeing how big a pumpkin they could pick up each year added to the excitement of picking out a pumpkin. Of course, Jake, or one of the other staff members, picked out pumpkins for the little ones that could not walk. No child was ever left out, regardless of how young they were.

When a pumpkin was picked out, the child's first name and last initial was written on it so there was no doubt as to what pumpkin belonged to whom. When they made it back to the orphanage, all of the pumpkins were lined up on the front porch. It was an exciting day when Mrs. Miller declared it would be pumpkin carving day. When this happened, you could hear shouts of joy and clapping in all of the school rooms. Mrs. Miller was always thankful when the weather cooperated and gave them an Indian Summer day.

When it was pumpkin carving day, all the staff members would spend the day with the children carving the pumpkins. Mrs. Miller would instruct the children to put on some old play clothes. It was a messy day, but so much fun! Pumpkin seeds would pop up in the strangest places for several days after pumpkin carving day. The chatter and laughter could be heard all over the grounds. Mrs. Miller was not sure who was having the most fun – the staff or the children.

Sometimes Jake and a couple of the other staff members could be seen carving pumpkins late at night after they got their work chores done. They never wanted any child to be without their very own pumpkin.

Once all of the pumpkins were carved, they were lined up on the front porch of the orphanage with the tiniest ones in the front row and the bigger ones in the back row. On Halloween night, you could look down the lane and see the twinkling of the candle lights in the pumpkins and see the faces that had been carved in them. It was never known how many children were at the orphanage, but it was assumed that if you counted the pumpkins you would have a good idea of how many children there were. The only problem with that theory was no one could get close enough to count the pumpkins!

The orphanage children never participated in traditional "trick or treating," but they did not miss out on any "treats" or any of the fun. Mrs. Miller, along with the rest of the staff, made sure of that. They spent many days before Halloween making goodie bags filled with candy and cookies for each child. On Halloween day, no school was held in the afternoon. If the weather cooperated, the children played special games in the yard and wore masks that they had made in their art classes. Jake took them for a ride up and down the lane in the cart that he had filled with straw. The day ended with warm apple cider and more cookies in front of a roaring fire in the house after supper time. If anyone thought that the orphanage children were deprived, they were sadly mistaken.

The church volunteers that worked in the pumpkin patch made sure that the kitchen workers at the orphanage had plenty of pumpkins to cook with. During the fall

HALLOWEEN PUMPKINS

months, right up to the first of the year, there was always someone in the kitchen creating sweet treats - pumpkin pies, pumpkin bread, pumpkin bars, pumpkin cookies, pumpkin butter. There was no end to their creativity. Even those staff members that did not participate in food preparation enjoyed helping that time of the year. It was a joy to hear the peals of laughter coming from the kitchen when the baking was taking place. The minute you walked into the front door of the orphanage on the baking days, the aroma of spices and sugar floated through the air. Your mouth would begin watering just thinking about the goodies that would be setting out on the counters. And, most days were baking days as long as they had pumpkins!

Jake loved to build things, so he built a stand on the side of the road coming into Calvary so that many of the sweet treats coming out of the orphanage's kitchen could be sold to those who came to visit the pumpkin patch. Even the locals would drive out to visit the stand to take home a goodie or two.

Jake had painted a large, wooden sign which he mounted on a stake driven into the ground in front of the road side stand - "Sugar Shack—Pumpkin Patch Goodies for Sale." The orphanage cooks had quite a reputation for baking the best pumpkin pies for miles around. Everyone in the area looked forward to taking something home in addition to their pumpkins for Jack-O-Lanterns.

After all the goodies were boxed up, Jake would get the wagon out again and transport the sweet treats to the stand. Each day, two of the older children were allowed to ride in the wagon and spend the morning or afternoon with

Jenny's Angel

a couple of the staff members at the stand as the sweet treats were sold. It was quite a treat to do this since they were excused from school for that time period. Mrs. Miller was happy to see the children participate and knew that this was a great learning experience for them. The children would take an inventory of what baked items they were loading in the wagon, keep track of what was sold, count out change to the customer when they sold an item, take an inventory of the left over items at the end of the day and count how much money they had made for the day. The children were learning how to operate a business while having fun. That was Mrs. Miller's goal.

When Jenny got old enough to participate, she was ecstatic. She loved being involved in every step of the process. She particularly liked riding in the wagon with Jake, arranging all the baked items in the stand and seeing all the visitors come to the stand to buy the goodies. Jenny was not bashful and would talk to anyone who stopped by. Whatever was being sold, Jenny would hand it to the customer, count out their change and reward them with a big dimpled smile. It did not take Jenny long to learn all the steps that were necessary to be able to be chosen to work at the stand. It was a fun day for her.

Mrs. Miller was so thankful for the funds that were raised from the sale of the baked goodies. They had no problem putting the funds to good use as there was never an abundance of funds. Mrs. Miller allotted a certain amount of what was raised every year to be spent for a special project. Each year before the pumpkins were harvested and the baking started, the staff and the children would gather in their dining room and come up with ideas of what to do

HALLOWEEN PUMPKINS

with the money raised at the Sugar Shack Pumpkin Patch Goodie stand. With Mrs. Miller's help, their list would get narrowed down and then eventually one project would be chosen. That would get everyone excited about the baking and the selling. The more goodies they baked, the more they could sell, the more money they would have!

Chapter 15

JENNY'S CRUTCH

By the time Jenny was ten years old, she looked like a china doll. She had blue eyes that sparkled when she smiled, golden hair that hung in ringlets and a peaches and cream complexion with big dimples, but Jenny was oblivious as to what a beautiful child she was. She was a good student, and even with her crooked foot, loved to run and play. She knew she could not do everything that the other children did that were not crippled, but it did not affect her disposition. She was always like the sunshine on a rainy day. She thumped along with the crooked foot, laughing and squealing along the way.

Jenny was happiest when she was outside in the sunshine even on days when it snowed. She would giggle as the wind blew through her golden curls, delighted in the birds as they sat in the trees singing their songs and laughed as the snowflakes landed on her eyelashes. Her laugh was infectious, and Mrs. Miller wondered if she was every going to outgrow the squealing sound she made when she was happy and excited.

Sometimes Jake would stand and watch the children playing outside, and he always looked for Jenny. He loved all the children and never showed any favoritism to Jenny, but she had stolen his heart when he first saw her in that basket. He knew that would never change. One day as she was slowly walking up the path to the porch, she winced as she walked on her crippled foot. Jake was so happy that

JENNY'S CRUTCH

Jenny had shoes and knew that they helped keep her foot warm and dry, but at times, he knew that her foot hurt. Jake had been thinking about making Jenny a crutch to use when her foot hurt, or at times when she needed a little extra support. When Jake saw Jenny that particular day, he was convinced that he needed to put his woodworking skills to use and make a crutch just for her.

Behind the orphanage, there was a footbridge that crossed the Calvary River. Most of the time there was not much water in the river. If there was a big rain, the water would rise and rush along the banks, but that usually happened in the spring or fall when there were more big rains. The yard of the orphanage was surrounded by a tall wrought iron fence so the staff members did not have to be concerned about the children being near the river. There were times when the staff took the children across the footbridge to the other side of the river, but the children never went by themselves.

On the other side of the footbridge, beyond the sandy beach along the river's edge, there was an area that was cleared of trees and beyond that was a dense forest of trees. Someone had put a large swing set, a teeter totter, a slide and a sandbox in the cleared area that ran along the sandy beach. Jake and everyone else assumed that the playground items were put there when the orphanage was being built. Close to the edge of the forest was a wooden bench.

The footbridge that crossed the river was not very wide and was made of wooden planks with a railing on each side of the bridge. It was a very special treat for the children from the orphanage to make the trek across the footbridge and play at the playground but, of course, they never ventured into the dense forest of trees. They were given very stern lectures about not going into the forest of trees and knew they would be disciplined if they even ventured close.

The older children made up stories about the forest of trees and creatures that lived in the forest. They told these stories to the younger children so most of the younger children did not venture very far off the playground when they were taken over to play. Most all the children enjoyed going over the footbridge to that side of the river though.

When Jake had free time, he quite often spent it making things out of wood or whittling. He was convinced he could make Jenny a crutch. All he needed to do was to find the perfect limb on a tree, and to do that, he would have to go to the forest across the footbridge. Jake took off late one afternoon and roamed around in the woods looking for the type of tree from which he could cut a branch to make a crutch. He had decided that the crutch should be made from a branch from a Hickory tree. It took Jake a couple of hours, but he finally found the perfect tree and the perfect branch. Whatever he made for Jenny had to be perfect! He had not brought a saw with him so he tied his red handkerchief around the branch. He was certain he could find the tree again. He would just have to make another trip into the woods with his saw. He was determined to make that crutch for Jenny.

Jake did not want anyone to know what he was up to so on his next day off, he disappeared into the woods

JENNY'S CRUTCH

again, this time with his saw. It did not take him long to find the Hickory tree with his red handkerchief tied onto it. He quickly sawed it off. It was an easy job as it would not take a very big limb to make a little crutch.

For the next several days, Jake spent all of his spare time in the shed behind the orphanage working on the crutch. He spent many hours using the wood rasp to change the limb into a crutch, and then, more hours sanding it down. The more it looked like a crutch, the more excited Jake got about making it. He was just sure that the little crutch would help Jenny's foot from getting as sore. He did not like to see Jenny in any discomfort.

Finally, the little crutch was shaped and sanded smooth. It was time to take it to Jenny. He had polished the wood, stained it and put a rubber cap on the end. But first Jake had to show Mrs. Miller what he had done and get her permission to give it to Jenny. He was not sure how she was going to react and was a little hesitant in approaching her. Jake wanted to make sure that Mrs. Miller was in her office when he approached her. He did not want anyone else around in case she was not happy at what he had done. He knew that she always went there after the supper hour. As soon as she headed that direction one evening, he went to his workshop and picked up the crutch. He felt his heart beating fast as he knocked on her door.

Mrs. Miller was astounded when she saw the crutch. It was a beautifully crafted little crutch. Jake had even padded the top of it so it would be soft under Jenny's arm. Mrs. Miller told Jake that the next morning after breakfast she would call Jenny into her office, and he could give the

Jenny's Angel

crutch to her. Jake was so relieved that Mrs. Miller was as excited as he was about Jenny having the crutch.

When Jenny went to the dining room the next morning, she was told that she was to go to Mrs. Miller's office after breakfast. Jenny's stomach did flip flops. She wondered if she was in trouble. No one ever got called to Mrs. Miller's office unless he or she was in trouble. Jenny could hardly eat her oatmeal for thinking about why she had to go to Mrs. Miller's office. When the other children headed to the school rooms, Jenny dawdled as long as she could and then hesitantly walked down the hall to Mrs. Miller's office. She was not very anxious to get there and wondered what was going to happen. Jake could hear the slow dragging sound of Jenny's foot so he knew she was on her way. Jake opened the door just as Jenny got to it.

Jenny looked up at Jake with a surprised look in her big blue eyes and whispered, "Mr. Jake, what are you doing here? Miss Elizabeth told me I was to go to Mrs. Miller's office after breakfast. Am I in trouble?"

Mrs. Miller stood up from behind her desk and smiled at Jenny as she said, "No, Jenny. You are not in trouble. Come on in. Mr. Jake has made something for you, and he wants to show it to you."

As Jenny came through the door Jake stepped behind her and held the crutch to his back so she would not see it. When Jenny looked around, Jake brought the crutch around so Jenny could see it. All she could do was stare at the crutch Jake was holding. Jake held the crutch out to Jenny and said, "Jenny, sometimes I know your foot hurts

JENNY'S CRUTCH

after you have run and played, and I thought maybe this might help."

Jenny did not make a move. She just stared at the crutch. Thoughts scrambled through Jake's mind – she does not like the crutch; she does not want to use a crutch; I have hurt her feelings. Now what do I say? Mrs. Miller was baffled at Jenny's reaction also.

All of a sudden, Jenny's face broke out into the most beautiful dimpled smile and her blue eyes sparkled. Out came one of her famous squeals. Relief washed over Jake's face. When Jenny squealed, Mrs. Miller and Jake knew that she was a happy little girl. She held out her hands for the crutch.

"Oh, Mr. Jake, you made a crutch for me? How did you know what size to make it?"

"Well, Jenny, I had to guess, so why don't you try it to see if it fits."

Jenny had never used a crutch, so at first, she was somewhat awkward, but it did not take long for her to master the use of it. She walked in circles around Mrs. Miller's desk and around Jake. Jake told her that she did not have to use it all the time, but when her foot was hurting, it might help. When Jenny let out one of her delightful laughs along with another squeal, Mrs. Miller and Jake knew that she would probably be taking her crutch with her everywhere, even if she did not use it.

Chapter 16

THE GARDEN

On one end of the orphanage grounds, there was a large garden plot and a stand of fruit trees. Not only did the fruit trees and garden produce an abundance of fruit and vegetables for the orphanage children to have at their meals, but it also served as a place for learning and another way to raise funds. Mrs. Miller was a strong believer in using the garden plot and fruit trees as a place for learning. The children learned how vegetables were grown and how the trees blossomed and produced fruit. In addition to having fresh vegetables and fruit fixed a multitude of ways, the garden also saved the orphanage money by not having to purchase those items. Those who tended to the garden tried to grow enough produce to put in the cellar for the winter months, or for the kitchen staff to can.

Some of the children loved to work in the garden, but some were not necessarily fond of eating the vegetables they helped produce! Mrs. Miller had a rule that they had to take at least one bite of whatever was being served. If they did not like it, they did not have to eat any more. She was a wise woman and knew that as the children grew into adulthood, they would learn to like many things that as a child, they would turn their noses up at. Mrs. Miller wanted meal time to be a happy time for the children so she did not press the issue of eating foods they did not like. Dr. Carlson always declared the children amazingly healthy and that was Mrs. Miller's goal.

THE GARDEN

All the children gathered in the dining room at the same time to have their meals together. When they heard the dinner bell, they knew it was meal time. The dining room was filled with round tables covered with tablecloths made of bright colored oil cloth. There were eight chairs around each table. Lined up against the wall at one end were a few high chairs for the babies and toddlers. Most of the time, the walls were decorated with art work made in the art classes.

Three times a year, a name card would be placed at each one of the chairs with a child's name on it. The children were always excited to see who they were going to sit with for that four month period of time. There would be a mix of older children and younger children sitting at each table. Mrs. Miller felt that this was one way to encourage the children to make friends of all ages and not always be with one small group.

At each meal, large bowls of food were set on the tables along with pitchers of milk and water. The older children were expected to help the younger children fill their plates, cut up their meat, pour their drink, butter their bread and be a good example with their manners. This gave the children a feeling of "family." There were always several staff members in the dining room to make sure that there was harmony at the table. Squabbles did not happen often, but just like in any family, they did happen.

Mrs. Miller never let an opportunity pass by where she could turn whatever they were doing into a learning session, and meal time was one of those opportunities. She felt that mealtime was an opportune time to teach them

Jenny's Angel

responsibility in caring for the smaller ones and how to cooperate with one another. Jenny loved to have the little ones sit at her table. She would act like a "little mother" to as many as would let her. Sometimes she would fuss over them a little too much.

When there were babies in the orphanage, Mrs. Miller encouraged the caretakers of the babies and the younger children who could not sit at the table and feed themselves to come to the dining room and feed them in their high chairs at one of the tables. She wanted everybody to feel like they were a part of the family, even the little ones.

Chapter 17

THE "BIGS" & THE "LITTLES"

If there was no one at Jenny's table that needed, or wanted her help, she would often gobble her food down and scurry over to where one of the babies were being fed. There was no end to Jenny's love for her "brothers and sisters." Jenny made up the name of "Bigs and Littles" to describe the other children, and it was not long before even the staff members would refer to the children in those terms. Just exactly at what age someone was no longer a "Little" and became one of the "Bigs" no one ever knew for sure.

Before every meal, all the children would hold hands around the table and say a short, simple prayer of thanks. Mrs. Miller, or one of the other staff members, would lead the prayer, but the children were expected to say it out loud also. It did not take the "Littles" long to learn the prayer. Mrs. Miller always asked the children if there was someone who wanted to lead the prayer. Sometimes there was a volunteer, and sometimes there was not, but that was OK. She encouraged even the littlest one to lead a prayer, even if he or she did not say it perfectly.

After being employed at the orphanage a short time, it did not take Mrs. Miller very long to believe that being the director of the orphanage was her calling in life. There was not a day that went by that she did not say a prayer of thanks for being given the opportunity to be able to spend, what she hoped would be, the rest of her days with the children at the orphanage. She was like Jake in that she had no children and was widowed. She loved all the children

Jenny's Angel

that came to the orphanage. When one was adopted out of the orphanage, it was a difficult time for her.

After the supper meal and plates were checked, the children were allowed to go to the large living room to read or to the playroom. If it was summer, and the days were still bright with sunlight, they would be given the opportunity to go outside to play. It was always their choice as to where they wanted to spend their evenings – inside or outside. Jenny almost always headed for the front door. She knew she could not run and jump like the other children, but she did not care. Sometimes she would grab her crutch and take off thumping across the wooden floor, and sometimes she skittered with her leather shoe slapping the floor. Everyone could tell by the sound how Jenny was making her way to the door.

One of the favorite games that the children played outside was dodge ball, but that was a difficult game for Jenny to play. She just could not maneuver her foot, or the crutch, quickly enough to get out of the way of the ball. But that did not bother Jenny. When they were playing that game, she would find another group to play with, or play by herself. Jenny never seemed to let much of anything put her in a bad mood.

When the days were filled with sunlight, the younger children, 5th grade and younger, were rounded up to go back inside at 7:00 p. m., while the older children were allowed to stay outside until 8:00 p. m. Jenny was thrilled when she made it to 6th grade and was able to stay outside with the "Bigs," as she called them. The staff members would take the "Littles" in and get them cleaned up and ready for bed. At 8:00, the "Bigs" would be called in for the same routine. By 9:00 p.m., all the children had to be in their rooms, and all lights were to be out by 10:00 p.m. Wake up time was 7:00 a.m. every morning except on Saturday and Sunday when they were allowed to sleep until 8:00 a.m. Mrs. Miller was quite strict about the schedule for the children.

Chapter 18

THE FOOTBRIDGE AND THE FOREST

Most of the children enjoyed their trek outside to work in the garden, but they always had the option of staying in their classroom and reading, except for certain days when it was used as part of their classroom learning. When it was time for Jenny's class to work in the garden, she was usually at the beginning of the line. She loved the sunshine and was fascinated by the way blooms would be on the vines and produce a vegetable. She would watch as the green growth broke through the top of the soil and get taller and taller. She would be delighted when the onion tops would break through the soil or a corn stalk would produce an ear of corn. No one ever wanted to stifle the curiosity of the children. She even liked to hoe out the weeds. Jake had made some tools with short handles so the children could walk along with one of the staff members and do the same task. Sometimes when the children came back into the house after being outside in the garden, they would have to go straight in and take a bath. No one minded how dirty the children got. It was all a learning experience.

Another one of the children's favorite activities was to go across the footbridge and play in the sand and on the playground equipment. They had playground equipment on the grounds of the orphanage, but for some reason, crossing the river on the footbridge was exciting. During the spring, summer and fall months when the weather was nice, the children were allowed to cross the footbridge quite often, but only when they were accompanied by their teacher, or one of the other staff members. They all shouted with joy when they were told that it would be part of their day......if they did all their school work and behaved!

Mrs. Miller left it up to the discretion of the teachers how often they took their classes to the playground, as long as they did not abuse the privilege. She cautioned all the teachers to impress upon the children that they were not to go into the forest of trees. No one other than Jake had ever ventured into the forest, and she certainly did not want a child to go exploring and become lost.

The older boys made up stories about the strange creatures and witches that lived in the forest and teased the younger children with these stories. They would tell the "Littles" that if they got too close to the forest, one of the creatures, or one of the witches, would grab them, and they would never be seen again. Mrs. Miller discouraged this behavior, but found it difficult to stop the stories from being circulated. The teachers tried to dispel any fears about the forest of trees that some of the smaller children had, but it sometimes was difficult to convince them that there were no strange creatures or witches in the forest. Not all of the "Littles" were convinced, and when they walked over the footbridge to the playground, they stayed as far away from the forest as they could. At least the teacher did not have to worry about them wandering into the forest and getting lost.

Jenny never listened to the stories and never thought the forest was a scary place. She thought making the trip across the footbridge to the playground was great fun and believed that the forest was a magical place. Even though

Jenny's Angel

Jenny was old enough to not believe in fairies or mystical beings, she loved to let her imagination roam and write or tell stories about the "enchanted forest." Her teacher, Miss Cartwright, wondered how she dreamed up some of these stories. Jenny had a very big imagination! If she could get some of the "Littles" to sit down and listen, she would read her stories to them, or make one up as they sat there.

All winter long, Jenny would look out the window toward the footbridge and forest and wish that spring would come so they could go across the footbridge to play. She would stand at the window and watch the snow flakes hit the window and turn into a drizzle down the window. As soon as the weather turned warm in the spring, she would beg Miss Cartwright to take them across the footbridge to the playground. Of course, the answer was always the same. They had to do their schoolwork first, and everyone had to behave, if they were to be allowed the privilege of going across the footbridge to the playground. Miss Cartwright was one of the youngest teachers, and everyone suspected that she enjoyed going to the playground across the footbridge as much as the children did.

Whenever Miss Cartwright took a class to the playground, she ran around with the children and played with them on the playground equipment. Those who watched the happy band of children and Miss Cartwright running around, with laughter filling the air, could not tell who was having the most fun. Miss Cartwright would often volunteer to take one of the other teacher's class across the footbridge while the teacher took care of Miss Cartwright's class. Most of the time, the other teachers were more than willing to take her up on her offer.

THE FOOTBRIDGE AND THE FOREST

The teachers at the orphanage were also employed at the orphanage during the summer months when the children were not in school. During June, July and August, the children did not have formal classes so the teachers involved them in activities that they never found time to do during the school year. They would do special art projects, get involved in building projects with Jake, enlist the cooks to give cooking lessons, do sewing projects, get involved in taking care of the yard and flowers, and these were the months that they spent the most time in the garden. The children were allowed to participate in the activities of their choice rather than a teacher choosing for them. The only requirement was that they had to be involved in the special project for at least two hours at a time. Sometimes a child would get so involved in a project that he or she did not want to quit for days or even weeks. It was amazing how the teachers were able to organize all of the projects and keep everyone happy, but they did it. Mrs. Miller would circulate and watch the children. She was so proud of her staff and pleased at how much fun the children had while learning as well as how they all cooperated with one another. Oh, yes, there were squabbles, and sometimes a few tears were shed, but after all, they were children.

Chapter 19

THE CORNER CAFÉ

Several times during the summer months, the children who were at least four years old would be allowed to participate in a field trip. Getting to go on a field trip was the best activity of all! Jake would get the car ready and a small group of the children would be taken into Calvary along with a staff member. Most days Jake would take more than one car load in a day. Mrs. Miller wanted all of the children to have this opportunity.

The children would walk up and down Main Street and look in the store windows. Their eyes would get wide at the vast array of items. Each trip they would be allowed to go into a couple of the stores to look at the merchandise. On the way home, they would talk excitedly about the merchandise they saw, what it cost and how it was bought to stock the shelves and then sold. This was another learning experience for the children although they thought it was great fun. Mrs. Miller wanted the children to get acclimated to being in the public and away from the orphanage. They would not always live in the orphanage, and she knew they had to learn about the outside world. She did not want them to be afraid to leave the orphanage. For several days after a field trip was taken, some of the younger children could be seen playing "store" and spending their play money.

The highlight of a field trip was a visit to the Corner Cafe in the middle of the afternoon when it was not busy. If Miss Callie had gone home for her afternoon nap, someone would hurry to her house and tell her the children were there. She never wanted to miss them and was as thrilled to see the children come into her restaurant as they were to be there. She fussed over them as if she was their grandma, and they all loved it. The children would take a seat at the tables, and Miss Callie would serve each of them a scoop of ice cream and one of her famous cookies. The next day, having the children come to the restaurant was all that she could talk about.

Other than going into Calvary, Jenny's most favorite activities were those that involved doing something outside – crossing the footbridge, working in the garden, helping with the flowers – anything to be outside. Her little arms and legs turned a golden tan and a few freckles popped out across her nose. Whenever she was outside and saw Mr. Jake, she would scamper though the grass and run up to his side. She would pull on his sleeve and give him one of her biggest smiles and, of course, he never failed to lovingly pull on her pony tail and give her a hug.

If you asked Jenny what her very favorite activity was, she never wavered in her answer. It was to cross the footbridge, play on the playground, in the sand and be near the forest. No one could figure out why Jenny loved that dense forest so much. Of course, she was never allowed to venture into it, but she never tired of looking into the trees and making up stories about the forest.

One sunny Saturday in May, Miss Cartwright told the children that she would take a group over in the morning and another group over in the afternoon. She made the announcement in the dining room just as the children were

Jenny's Angel

finishing their breakfast. When she asked who would like to go that morning, Jenny's hand was the first one that shot up. She would go both times if Miss Cartwright would let her, but she knew that was not going to happen.

After Miss Cartwright had the children divided into the morning and afternoon groups, she told the morning group to put their play clothes on and gather on the front porch. Jenny was going to be in the morning group so she shot out of her chair and headed toward her room just as soon as she was excused from the table. She had plenty of old clothes to put on to go to the playground. Every year at Christmas time and at Easter, each child was given two new outfits of clothes that was chosen especially for them. The rest of their clothes were hand-me-downs that had been outgrown by the other children. Mrs. Miller was never quite sure where the money was going to come from each year for the new clothes, but her faith was strong. And, she never had to disappoint any of the children.

Chapter 20

THE OLD MAN

Jenny rummaged through her drawer looking for some play clothes. When she was dressed, she hurriedly made it to the porch. She did not want to be late and miss out on the trip over the footbridge. It did not take very long for all the children to gather on the porch, so off they went singing a song as they marched along.

The teachers and staff members always cautioned the children to walk, and not run, when they crossed the footbridge and to stay in the center. They were not to hang onto the wooden rail that was on each side of the bridge, but were supposed to hold the hand of one other person. If the boards were wet, they could be rather slippery.

Once the children made it across the footbridge, it did not take long for them to scatter throughout the playground and up and down the little beach area by the river or in the sandbox. Rarely did the river have enough water in it to be concerned about anyone drowning in it. If there was only one staff member or teacher, no more than eight or ten children were taken over at a time, so that it would not be difficult to keep track of them.

Jenny headed for the swing set and suddenly stopped. An old wooden bench had always been sitting not too far from the forest of trees. The children knew that the bench was as far as they were to venture since the forest was behind it. Once in a while, the teacher would sit on it for a

Jenny's Angel

few minutes and watch the children.

Jenny stood and stared at the bench. She was mesmerized by what she saw. No one else seemed to notice. There on the bench was an old man wearing a raggedy looking coat. Even though he was sitting down, to Jenny he looked like he was a very big man. One of his large gnarled hands was wrapped around a long piece of wood that looked like a staff. He was sitting very quietly. His hair was white and a little bit scraggly. As Jenny stood staring at the old man, he looked directly at her and smiled. Jenny smiled back and turned to see where Miss Cartwright was.

She saw Miss Cartwright at the other end of the playground. Evidently Jenny was the only one that was paying any attention to the old man sitting on the bench. Jenny scampered over to Miss Cartwright as quickly as her little crippled foot would allow. She tugged on Miss Cartwright's sleeve and said, "Look at the bench. There is an old man sitting on it. He smiled at me." Miss Cartwright's first thought was that Jenny was teasing her, or letting her imagination roam again.

Miss Cartwright followed Jenny's gaze to the park bench, and sure enough, there was an old man in a raggedy coat sitting on the park bench. Miss Cartwright was baffled. Where did he come from? Who was he? No one had ever been seen on this side of the footbridge. Was there a house somewhere beyond the forest? Or, in the forest?

At first, Miss Cartwright did not know what to do. He looked rather old, so surely he would not harm the children. None of them even seemed to take notice of

THE OLD MAN

the old man except Jenny. She did not want to scare the children so she whispered to Jenny, "Just go and play. Do not pay any attention to the old man, and do not go over to the bench. Pretend like he is not there."

Jenny followed Miss Cartwright's instructions, but she had a hard time not looking at the old man. She tried her hardest not to look in his direction, but she just did not seem to be able to stop. She was spellbound by him. Every time she looked at the old man, he would look right into her eyes and smile at her. His eyes would crinkle up on the corners when he smiled. Jenny thought he looked like a kindly, old gentlemen and wondered if he was lonely sitting all by himself, but Miss Cartwright had given her strict instructions not to pay an attention to him. She did not want to get into trouble and not be able to make trips across the footbridge.

When it was time to go back across the footbridge, Miss Cartwright gathered up the children and headed back for lunch. She tried not to pay any attention to the old man, but it was rather difficult, knowing he was sitting there. She wondered if the old man would be there in the afternoon when she brought the other group of children over. She was anxious to get back to tell Mrs. Miller about the old man. As Jenny lined up with the other children, she took one last look at the old man and raised her hand in a little wave. The old man raised his hand and waved back at Jenny. Oh, she wanted so badly to go over and talk to him. She hoped he would be there the next time she came back to play.

When Miss Cartwright told Mrs. Miller about the old man, Mrs. Miller was just as baffled and somewhat concerned. She did not know where the old man could have come from. She thought that the forest of trees was very large, so if anyone had come from the other side, they would have had to walk for a very long way. After mulling this over for a while, she decided she would send Jake into town to make some inquiries of the town folk to see if they knew who the old man was or where he came from. Her primary responsibility at all times was to keep the children safe.

The teachers and staff members continued taking small groups of the children across the bridge to the playground several times during the week once school was out. They were all totally baffled by the fact that when Jenny was in the group, the old man was always sitting on the bench in the same position, and when she was not in the group, he was not there. When Jenny would look at the old man, he would smile, and of course, Jenny always flashed her big dimpled smile at him. The old man always had his raggedy coat on and had the staff in his gnarled hand. He never got up off the bench, nor did he try to talk to them.

The old man seemed quite harmless, and eventually no one paid much attention to him as he sat quietly on the bench. The children were told not to approach him, so before long, they just ignored his presence. Jake's trip into town to ask about the old man did not result in any information. No one knew for sure, but everyone just assumed that he was from the other side of the forest and enjoyed watching the children. This was not quite a satisfactory answer for Mrs. Miller, but she did not pursue the situation any further. The area across the footbridge did not belong to the orphanage so he had a right to sit on the bench.

THE OLD MAN

After seeing the old man a few times, Jenny started begging Miss Cartwright to let her go to say "hi" to the old man. Miss Cartwright's answers were always the same. "No you cannot go over to the old man. Just go play." Jenny would look wistfully at the old man. Finally, one day, after Jenny pleaded with Miss Cartwright for several minutes, she finally gave in. She thought that maybe if she let Jenny go once, she would be satisfied and not ask to go again.

After Jenny's pleading session, Miss Cartwright told Jenny that she would walk over with her, and she could say "Hi" to the old man. Miss Cartwright took Jenny's hand while Jenny excitedly scuttled up to the bench with her crutch dragging in the sand. Jenny was not at all afraid of the old man and stood right in front of him. Miss Cartwright was just a few feet away.

Chapter 21

CHRISTOPHER

"Hi," Jenny said. "What is your name?"

The old man looked steadily at Jenny with his piercing blue eyes and with a smile said, "My name is Christopher and you, little miss, are called Jenny."

Jenny's eyes got bigger and said, "How did you know my name? How do you know me?"

The old man's eyes twinkled as he grinned and pondered Jenny's questions as he scratched his chin.

"Well, Jenny. I have known you since you came to live in the orphanage when you were a little baby."

"You have? Are you my grandpa? You have blue eyes that look like mine. I don't have a grandpa, but I would like to have one. Sometimes I call Mr. Jake 'grandpa', but he is really Mr. Jake."

The old man chuckled, as he replied, "No, Jenny, I am not your grandpa."

"Then why are you here? Why do you just sit on this bench every day?"

"I am here for you, Jenny. I will be here whenever you need me."

CHRISTOPHER

Jenny was puzzled and was about to ask another question when she heard Miss Cartwright call her name and motion for her to come. She quickly turned away and started to scamper back to the playground, but stopped and looked over her shoulder and said, "Will you be here when I come back to play another day?"

"Yes, Jenny, I will be here when you come back to play."

As Jenny headed back to the swings, she was very confused. The old man knew her name and said that he was "there for her." What did that mean? Miss Cartwright was standing within hearing distance. Maybe she would know what the old man meant. Jenny had been told the story about how she had been found in a basket at the gate when she was a tiny baby, but she never thought much about it. She was happy to be at the orphanage. Jenny wondered if the old man knew who had left her at the orphanage. He said he knew her when she was a little baby. None of this made any sense to Jenny, but she knew that she liked the old man. She was sure that he was a very special old man. She hoped he would be on the bench the next time she came over to play. She wanted to talk to him some more.

Miss Cartwright had heard the conservation between Jenny and the old man, and she was as baffled as she knew that Jenny must be. The old man did nothing that made her afraid, but it was a very baffling situation. None of it made any sense to her. She, too, wondered if the old man had known who put Jenny in the basket at the gate of the orphanage. She wondered also if Jenny had thought about this. She did not want to discuss any of her thoughts

Jenny's Angel

with Jenny. She would have to tell Mrs. Miller about Jenny's encounter as soon as she got back.

The rest of the day was uneventful for Jenny, and she did not talk about the old man named Christopher, but she kept thinking about him. That evening, Mrs. Miller came to her room and sat down on the corner of Jenny's bed.

"Did you have fun today, Jenny?"

"Oh, yes, Mrs. Miller. I always like to go over the footbridge to the playground. I love to be near the forest and the river. It is my favorite thing to do."

"Did you talk to the old man that was sitting on the bench?"

Jenny began to wonder if she was in trouble. She hesitated and then said, "Yes. I asked him what his name was, and he said it was Christopher."

"Did he say where he lived?"

"No, Mrs. Miller. I did not ask him where he lived. I did not get to talk to him very long because Miss Cartwright called for me to come."

"OK, Jenny. You have a good night's rest and say your prayers before you go to sleep."

Mrs. Miller did not want to question Jenny too much. She did not want to make Jenny afraid to talk to her about the old man. She just wanted to see if Jenny expressed

CHRISTOPHER

anything about the old man that she did not already know. She knew what Jenny's conversation had been with the old man, because Miss Cartwright had heard it and had told her about it.

Jenny was glad that Mrs. Miller did not ask her any more questions. She knew that whatever Mrs. Miller asked, she had to tell the truth. She wanted her conversation with the old man to be her secret, although she knew that Miss Cartwright was standing close by and probably heard what they said. She wondered if he would be there when she crossed the footbridge the next time she went over to play. Even though she had a very short conversation with the old man, Christopher, Jenny felt like she had made a new friend, and that made her smile. Jenny went to sleep thinking about the old man and drifted in and out of dreams about her day.

Chapter 22

A COOKIE FOR CHRISTOPHER

Jenny, along with all the other children, spent the summer playing in the yard, working in the garden, going to the pumpkin patch to observe the growth of the pumpkins and working on all kinds of projects. They were so excited when the first baby pumpkins began to be seen on the vines.

There was a lot of rain during those summer months which made the water in the Calvary River rise to the point that it was quite deep in many areas and lapped up on the banks. When the children crossed the footbridge to go to the playground, they were always reminded to be very careful.

Each time that Jenny was with the group that crossed over, the old man was sitting quietly on the bench. He was always sitting in the same spot holding the staff in front of him. This perplexed Mrs. Miller and all of the staff. This was something that they did not discuss in front of Jenny, or any of the other children, but it was quite often a topic of conversation.

The children had never paid much attention to the old man and as the days went by, never even looked his way. He never said anything to any of them, but just sat quietly watching when Jenny was in the group. Even though it was summer time, the old man always had the raggedy coat on. Jenny was always excited to see him and begged to be

A COOKIE FOR CHRISTOPHER

allowed to go over and talk to him. It was a mystery to everyone as to why Jenny was so drawn to the old man.

If any of the children asked Jenny why she talked to the old man, she would tell them that Christopher was her friend, but said little more. Several of the boys teased her about being friends with an old man that wore a raggedy coat. There was hardly anything that would make Jenny angry, but she would get upset when anyone said anything unkind about Christopher. She would get a frown on her face, stomp her little crippled foot on the ground and tell everyone he was a nice man, and that his name was Christopher. She did not like for them to call him an old man.

Mrs. Miller told the staff members to let Jenny talk to the old man for a short period of time, if she asked. Mrs. Miller did not want to make too much of a fuss about it. She was sure that Jenny's interest in the old man would soon wane. Much to the surprise of everyone, that did not happen.

One day as they were almost finished with lunch, Jenny grabbed Mrs. Miller's hand as she walked by and said that she had a question. She whispered so quietly that Mrs. Miller had to bend down to hear what Jenny was saying. She got as close as she could to Mrs. Miller's ear and asked if she could take a cookie to Christopher just in case he was sitting on the bench when they took the trip over the footbridge that afternoon. Jenny did not want any of the other children to hear her because she was afraid they would tease her. They told her he was just a wrinkled, old man. Mrs. Miller did not want to encourage Jenny to spend time with the old

Jenny's Angel

man, but yet, she always taught the children to be kind to others so it was difficult for her to tell Jenny that she could not take a cookie to the old man. Mrs. Miller also did not want Jenny to feel like she was apprehensive about letting her take a cookie to him.

After pondering this for a minute, she told Jenny that, yes, she could take a cookie to the old man, but she was not to stay long with him. She reminded Jenny that she was going across the bridge to play at the playground and in the sand. When Jenny heard Mrs. Miller reply, she was so excited she could hardly eat the rest of her lunch. Jenny very carefully wrapped the cookie in a napkin and put it in her pocket. She did not want it to get dirty or break apart.

After being dismissed from lunch, Jenny rushed out to the yard to wait for Miss Cartwright to take them across the footbridge. She was so anxious to see Christopher and give him the cookie, she could hardly stand still. When they reached the top of the footbridge, Jenny looked over the rail and there sat Christopher. As soon as they were across the bridge, the other children scattered around the playground equipment, but instead of heading to the swing set like she usually did, she told Miss Cartwright that Mrs. Miller said she could give a cookie to Christopher. After getting permission from Miss Cartwright, Jenny hobbled over to the bench.

The old man watched every step Jenny made as she came toward him. When she got close enough for her to hear, he smiled and said, "Hi Jenny. How are you today?"

Jenny answered, "I am just fine," as she dug the

cookie out of her pocket. "I have a cookie for you." She held her hand toward the old man.

The old man took the cookie and said to Jenny, "It is very nice that you brought a cookie for me. I know it will be delicious. Thank you very much. I will eat it later."

Jenny stared at him for a minute and said, "I can't stay, but I am glad to see you. I have a question to ask you. Where do you live?"

The old man motioned back toward the woods and said, "I live over through the forest."

Jenny was bewildered by his answer. Was there a house in the forest? Or did he live on the other side? Jenny did not have time to ask any more questions because the teacher was calling for her to come back to the playground. Jenny quickly said goodbye and hobbled back to the swings. As Jenny made her way, she remembered the stories the older boys were always telling about the forest when they wanted to scare the "Littles." She knew there were no goblins or witches in the forest, but wondered about the old man. Why was he always on the bench? He was friendly and always smiled at her. She knew that there was something special about Christopher, but she did not know what it was or why she thought that. She knew that when she saw him, it made her day special.

When she got back to the playground, the teacher asked her what the old man had said. Jenny told her that Christopher said thank you for the cookie and said he lived in the forest. Jenny then ran off to play with the other

Jenny's Angel

children. The teacher was as perplexed as Jenny was, but she did not say anything else to Jenny. The old man never did anything except sit on the bench so there was nothing to complain about. She would have liked to ask him why he was only on the bench when Jenny was in the group, but Mrs. Miller had given explicit instructions that no one was to approach the old man.

It rained for several days, and the children were not able to go outside to play. The staff tried to keep them busy with games they could play inside. They read books to the little ones and got some involved in making cookies in the kitchen. Sometimes they were not sure how many cookies actually made it onto the platters. Quite a few landed on the floor! At 3:00 p. m. on the days that cookies were made, the bell would ring and all the children knew it was time for warm cookies and a glass of cold milk. That was their treat for being good when they had to stay inside because of the bad weather.

Finally, the morning sunshine broke through the clouds. As they parted, a brilliant, blue sky was revealed. They were all hoping that the rain was over for awhile, but there were still some worrisome looking clouds hanging around. As the children entered the dining room for breakfast, they clapped their hands and jumped up and down and excitedly asked, "Can we go outside? Can we go to the playground? Can we? Can we?"

Jenny was not as boisterous as some of the children, but that day, she was so excited about being able to go outside that she was as loud as anyone. She was anxious to go back over the footbridge to see if Christopher would be on the bench. She hoped that he had stayed in his house on the rainy days. On those rainy days that they had to stay inside, sometimes Jenny would be seen standing at the window looking outside toward the footbridge.

Mrs. Miller told the children to sit down and eat their breakfast. She assured them that she would talk to the teachers, and they would decide what the activities would be for the day. She knew the children had been cooped up many days and were full of unspent energy. Even the older children were eager to be out of the house. Most of them were easier to occupy on rainy days as they were better at occupying themselves. It was the littler ones that were harder to keep occupied.

Mrs. Miller did not want to tell them they could not go outside, but, yet, she knew that it was very wet. Someone was sure to ask if they could go across the river, and that someone was probably going to be Jenny. She knew that the playground sand across the footbridge would not be good to play in. What a dilemma! If the children did go across the footbridge, they would have to put on their very oldest play clothes and shoes. After pondering it for a while and talking to the teachers, they all decided that the children did need to go outside for a little while. There was just too much pent up energy. Miss Cartwright volunteered to take a group over the footbridge to the playground and would do her best to keep the children off the beach area. Mrs. Miller sensed that Miss Cartwright needed to get outside and play too!

When Mrs. Miller went back to the dining room and told the children they could go outside, they all clapped and

Jenny's Angel

shouted. She gave them instructions about putting on their oldest play clothes and shoes. She said that a small group could go to the playground with Miss Cartwright and asked who wanted to go. Of course, Jenny's hand shot up high in the air before anyone else had their hands up. Most of the children did not care whether they went across to the playground or outside to play games, so Jenny got her wish. Jenny was going to be allowed to go with the small group that was going over the footbridge, and she was ecstatic!

Jenny most always ate all her breakfast, but she knew that she wanted to take something to Christopher. Before Jenny left the dining room, she wrapped up a small sweet roll in her napkin and took it to her room. She picked out a pair of pants that had a pocket it them so she could put the sweet roll in it. If Christopher was sitting on the bench, she wanted to have something to give to him. She was so excited and in such a hurry that she put her pants on backwards. She realized it when she tried to put the sweet roll in the pocket. So, then she had to take the time to take her shoes off and turn her pants around. Oh, she worried that she was going to be late, and they would leave without her. She ran out of the room with her bad foot thumping loudly on the wooden floor and bumped into Mrs. Miller.

"Young lady, where are you going in such a hurry?"

Jenny came to an abrupt stop, "Oh, I'm sorry. I was going to meet Miss Cartwright and go over the footbridge. I don't want to be late."

"Well, slow down, Jenny. Miss Cartwright is not going to leave without you. Where is your crutch? I think you should take it because the boards on the footbridge will be wet. I want you to be very careful."

Jenny's foot was rather stiff this morning, but she did not want Mrs. Miller to know. She was afraid that Mrs. Miller might tell her she could not go across the footbridge to the playground, and she just had to go over to see if Christopher was on the bench. Jenny hurriedly went back to her room, got her crutch and headed down the hall to find Miss Cartwright and the other children.

Chapter 23

CHRISTOPHER'S PROMISE

As the group approached the footbridge, Miss Cartwright could see that the Calvary River was very high and flowing very fast. She had never seen that much water in the river. There were a lot of branches, sticks, and other debris being carried along in the muddy water. With all of the rain that had fallen during the last few days, they were fortunate that the river had stayed within its banks and did not flood the pumpkin patch or the playground. It would be a tragedy if the pumpkin patch was destroyed.

The boards on the footbridge were still wet and slick, but all of the children held hands and made it across safely. They were so excited to be outside they quickly scattered in all directions, all but Jenny. As she stepped cautiously off the footbridge, she looked toward the bench, and sure enough, there was Christopher sitting in his raggedy coat, holding his staff. Jenny was so thrilled she could hardly keep from running over to the bench. Jenny looked expectantly at Miss Cartwright who knew immediately what Jenny wanted to do. She nodded her head at Jenny, but kept her eye on Jenny as she made her way over to the bench. Miss Cartwright slowly walked to the edge of the playground to be closer to Jenny as she approached the old man.

Miss Cartwright was as baffled as the rest of the staff and could not understand why Jenny was so drawn to the old man, but she did not say anything to her to stop her from going to talk to him. Mrs. Miller assured them that Jenny would tire of the old man eventually if they did not make a fuss about it, but that did not seem to be happening. It seemed that Jenny was more enthralled than ever. Miss Cartwright never got too far from Jenny and the old man, although she was sure that he was harmless. He had been there all summer and never even tried to talk to the children or the staff. He appeared to be very old. His face was craggy with deep wrinkles. She wondered how he even wandered through the woods from his house.

Miss Cartwright watched as Jenny sat down by the old man, something she had never done before. She watched Jenny pull something out of her pocket. She knew that Jenny was a very generous, caring youngster and was sure she had brought something from the breakfast table for the old man.

Jenny saw Miss Cartwright watching her and gave a little wave to her. She turned to the old man and said, "Hi. How are you today? I am glad you are here."

With a smile, the old man turned his head to look at Jenny and said, "I am just fine, Jenny."

Jenny looked intently into his eyes and said, "I remember your name is Christopher. If you live in the woods, does your family live with you? I have something for you. I brought you my sweet roll from breakfast. I hope you like it."

As she handed the sweet roll to Christopher, he took it from Jenny's hand and said, "Thank you, Jenny. You are a very special young lady."

Jenny's Angel

"How do you know I am special? I have a crippled foot. I cannot run as fast as the others, but that is OK. I like to play. I have lots of fun. Mr. Jake made this crutch just for me."

Christopher smiled and said, "Mr. Jake is a very kind man."

Christopher looked at Jenny and said, "I know you have a cripple foot, Jenny, but some day your foot will be well. I will always be here for you, Jenny."

Jenny was baffled at what Christopher had said. What did he mean when he said he was going to be there for her? And, he said her foot would be well. She knew that her crippled foot would never be like her good foot. She was perplexed and was about to ask him what he meant when she heard Miss Cartwright calling for her to come and play.

Oh how she wanted to sit on the bench and talk to Christopher, but knew that she had to listen to Miss Cartwright. She wanted to get to know Christopher better. Her mind was full of questions to ask him, but she never got to sit with him long enough to ask the questions. Even though the other children made remarks about how he looked just like a ragged old man, Jenny did not care. He was not just a raggedy old man. She knew he was an extraordinary person.

"Jenny," Christopher said, "Run and play with the other children. I will be here."
Jenny smiled her biggest dimpled smile and said

good-by to Christopher. She hopped off the bench and headed toward the swing set, dragging her crutch. She turned around and gave a little wave to the old man, which he returned with a smile.

Jenny loved to fly through the air in the swings as her hair blew all around her face, if it was not pulled back into a pony tail. She closed her eyes and pumped the swing to go higher and higher, letting the breeze cool her face. The other children were running around the playground, sliding on the slide and playing on the monkey bars, but she was content in the swing. Miss Cartwright glanced over at the old man on the bench occasionally. His eyes never seemed to leave Jenny.

Chapter 24

JENNY'S PLUNGE

Even though the sky had been a brilliant blue when they crossed the bridge, dark clouds were beginning to sneak across the sky, moving rapidly in their direction. There had been torrents of rain the past few days, and Miss Cartwright was not looking forward to another round of thunderstorms. She decided it was time to gather the children and head back across the footbridge before they got caught in the rain. As the sky began to darken, she called to the children to hurry and form a line so they could cross the footbridge. All the children jumped off the playground equipment and hurried toward Miss Cartwright. Jenny had to get her swing to stop, and then she had to grab her crutch. By the time she headed towards the other children, Miss Cartwright was hollering for her to hurry. Jenny scurried as fast as she could and looked over her shoulder to see if Christopher was still on the bench. As she glanced over, Christopher raised his bony hand in the air with a wave and smiled at her.

The first two in the line had started over the bridge as Jenny hobbled up behind the last one. Miss Cartwright was encouraging them to go as fast as they could, but to be careful on the slippery, wet boards. Big splats of rain began to fall, and the wind was whipping the tree branches.

Oh my, thought Miss Cartwright, *I should have gotten these children over the bridge sooner. This storm popped up so quickly, I did not see it coming. We will all be soaked by*

JENNY'S PLUNGE

the time we get to the house.

The rain began to fall steadily and the wind began to howl. Suddenly, one of the little girls slipped and fell down. Miss Cartwright quickly grabbed her hand to pull her up. She yelled at the children to hold tightly to their partner's hand and go as fast as they could. With the rain and the wind so strong, she wanted desperately to go back to the end of the line where Jenny was. As she turned, she saw Jenny's little crutch fly up in the air. In the blink of an eye, Jenny lurched forward. As soon as her body hit the slats, they broke. It looked like Jenny was airborne between the slats on the railing and fell over the side. Miss Cartwright screamed as she saw Jenny plunge into the water below. The river was swollen from the recent rains and was flowing very rapidly. Miss Cartwright felt like she was moving in slow motion.

Those children in front of Jenny began screaming, and two little girls burst out crying. Miss Cartwright yelled at them to hold tight to each other and to get across the footbridge. The rain pelted her face as she ran back down the footbridge. She had to get down to the edge of the river and see what happened to Jenny. Under the footbridge, there were large rocks that were slippery from the slime and moss that had accumulated on them. As she climbed over the rocks and looked down the river, she saw Jenny several yards beyond her. The river was flowing rapidly and Jenny was being carried downstream away from her. She could see Jenny's head bobbing in the water and an arm fly up into the air. She had to rescue Jenny! But how was she going to do it?

Jenny's Angel

    Miss Cartwright glanced quickly back at the other end of the bridge. She could see the children running up through the yard toward the house. As she did this, her mind was racing. She either had to run down the river's bank to try to catch up with Jenny, or she had to get into the river and hope she could swim with the current and catch up with Jenny. As she started to kick off her shoes and jump in the river, she took one last look and saw the old man running down to the river's edge. As he ran, he jerked off his heavy, ragged coat, threw it on the ground and waded into the river. Within a split second, the river engulfed him, and she could barely see where he was in the river. Miss Cartwright was stunned to see the old man move so nimbly and fast. She was even more surprised to see how quickly he was in the water and swimming in the same direction as Jenny. How could that old man accomplish that feat? She could not see where Jenny was nor could she see the old man. The rain was coming down in sheets.

    Miss Cartwright was almost paralyzed with fear for Jenny and the old man. She ran down the river's edge in the same direction that the current was taking them. She looked down the river and could see Jenny's head bobbing up and down and saw her hand reach up for a large piece of debris. The current was very strong due to all of the rains that had occurred, and there were all sizes and shapes of debris floating in the water. As she ran along the edge of the river, she prayed that neither one of them would get hit by something in the water.

    Miss Cartwright's heart was beating so fast she thought her chest would burst. Her tears mixed in with the rain as it assailed her face. With all of the logs, limbs and other debris in the water, and the current carrying the old man and Jenny downstream, she was so frightened she could hardly get her thoughts together. She knew that it would be no use for her to try to save Jenny from the river. She was not that strong of a swimmer, and the current was much too strong.

      What seemed like hours, but yet, was only minutes, there were other staff streaming across the yard of the orphanage paying no heed to the rain. The children had run into the house screaming that Jenny had fallen into the river. They were all trying to talk at once which made it difficult for anyone to understand what they were saying. Finally Mrs. Miller got one of the older boys to calm down enough to piece together the story and figure out what had happened. Several of the staff members ran out the door and headed to the footbridge, while others tried to calm the children.

      As they got to the base of the footbridge, they could see that Miss Cartwright was down the river bank, but had turned and was running back in their direction. She ran across the footbridge and met Jake. Rain was still pouring down and the wind was whipping her wet hair across her face. She did not know what Jake was going to do. She saw Jake suddenly stop and pick up Jenny's crutch. Oh, her heart ached for him, because she knew that Jenny was so special to him. He had just given her a new crutch a few days before, because she had outgrown the other one he had made. Jake grabbed Miss Cartwright's arm, and she could feel the silent sobs racking his body. He was yelling at her to tell him what happened, and in between sobs, all she could say was Jenny fell.

Jenny's Angel

Jake took Miss Cartwright back to the orphanage side. Everyone was in a state of panic, and no one knew what to do. Someone shouted that Mrs. Miller had called the fire department as soon as she heard that Jenny had fallen into the river. Miss Cartwright was so winded she could hardly talk, but kept saying over and over, "Jenny - The old man - The river" No one knew what she meant. All of a sudden, Miss Cartwright felt like a rock was sitting on her chest, and everything was beginning to move in slow motion around her. Then everything went black, and she fell to the ground as she fainted.

Everyone gathered around Miss Cartwright and all were talking at once. Why was she talking about the old man? They knew Jenny had fallen into the river, but what did the old man have to do with it. Jake had heard what Miss Cartwright had mumbled, but it made no sense. Jake was so stunned to think that Jenny had fallen into the river that he could hardly think straight. Scrambled thoughts kept rolling around in his mind, none of them making any sense. How could Jenny have fallen off of the footbridge? Was there something wrong with the crutch that made her fall? It must have been his fault! How could his little Jenny be carried away down the river? Why was Miss Cartwright mumbling about the old man?

As Jake looked down the river, he could see nothing except rocks and tree limbs in the swollen river. Jenny could not have fallen into the river. That was impossible. She was not tall enough to fall over the rail. But, where was she? Everyone was soaked from the rain, and no one seemed to be able to make a decision. Jenny was in the river, and Miss Cartwright was on the ground in a faint!

JENNY'S PLUNGE

Mrs. Miller was quick to assess the situation and started giving orders for someone to run to the house and get some blankets for Miss Cartwright who was beginning to rouse. Jake was in such a stupor he felt utterly useless. The only thing he could think to do was to go back across the footbridge and run down the bank to see if he could see Jenny. Maybe she would be clinging to a low branch. He had to do something to try to find her.

Jake knew that the firemen would be coming soon, but he wished they would hurry. Fortunately, the rain was beginning to slack off, and the wind had stopped blowing, but the river was still flowing rapidly. Jake pulled the bill of his cap down and took off across the footbridge again traveling as fast as he could, praying for a miracle. He had no idea how long Jenny had been in the river, but he had to try to find her. He was not giving up on Jenny. He believed in miracles, and he sure needed one now!

As Jake ran across the footbridge as quickly as he could, he glanced at the playground and the forest of trees. Even though his mind was in a turmoil and full of grief, he could not help but think about how Jenny loved crossing the footbridge, playing on the swing set and her love of the forest. Just thinking about it brought on a fresh round of tears. There was the bench in front of the forest. He knew that Jenny had become friends with an old man that sat on that bench every time she crossed over the footbridge.

Chapter 25

JENNY'S MIRACLE

As Jake neared the end of the footbridge, something caught his attention as he glanced at the bench. With his eyes full of tears, he could hardly make out anything, but he thought he saw something on the bench. He wiped his eyes and squinted as he looked. There was something on that bench! No one else had crossed the footbridge so what could it be? His eyesight was not very good, and he could not make out what it was. As far as he knew, the old man was the only one that ever used the bench by the forest. He was torn – should he take the time to investigate what was on the bench, or should he head down the river bank in the direction the river was flowing? It did not make any sense, but Jake felt an urgency to run over to the bench. It was like he was being pulled toward the bench.

The rain had slacked off considerably and was not much more than a heavy sprinkle. As Jake looked back at the staff members who were in the orphanage yard, he could see that no one else was coming across the footbridge. He looked down the river bank and then again at the bench. He did not have time to tarry. His mind was scrambling to make sense of his thoughts. He knew only minutes had passed, but it felt like hours. Jenny's life was at stake! But, he just had to see what was on that bench. Something was urging him to go in that direction. He raced across the playground as fast as he could. The closer he got the faster his heart beat. He could not run very fast, and his feet felt like they had twenty pound weights on them. He was sure

JENNY'S MIRACLE

he was running in slow motion. He had a strange tingling sensation the closer he got to the bench. He wondered if he was going to pass out, but he had to keep going. There was definitely an object laying on the bench! Was that a foot sticking up in the air? How could a body be on the bench? Was it his Jenny on that bench? How could it be? She was in the river. He must be going crazy!

As Jake got closer to the bench, he began to realize that there was a small body on it. How could a body be on that bench? There was no one on this side of the footbridge except Jenny. It had to be Jenny on the bench! But, Miss Cartwright had seen Jenny fall into the river.

By the time Jake reached the bench, he was so winded, he was gasping for his breath. His chest hurt, and he felt dizzy. He dropped to his knees, and for several seconds just stared at the child laying on the bench. It was his Jenny! He reached up and gently touched her cheek and softly said her name. How did she get on the bench? Was she alive? Her eyes were closed, and she felt cold. As he touched her cheek again and said her name, her eyelids fluttered. Jake's heart lurched. She was alive. Tears of happiness welled up in his eyes, and he felt like shouting.

Jenny was smeared with mud, her hair was matted with leaves and pieces of sticks were entwined in the curls. A bruise was beginning to form on her forehead. He did not see any other major cuts or bruises. When Jake looked down at her foot, he saw that she had lost the shoe off her crippled foot. That was OK. They could always get another shoe, but they could not get another Jenny!

Jenny's Angel

Jenny was laying on something that looked like a shabby, rumpled coat. Jake could not fathom where that came from, but it was soaked and he could not wrap Jenny in it. Even though his coat was wet, he jerked it off and spread it over Jenny. The inside of his coat was still dry so it would help a little.

"Little Miss Jenny. Jenny, it's me, Mr. Jake."

Jenny's eyes fluttered open as she mumbled, "Christopher, where is Christopher?"

Jenny's eyes fell shut again. Jake knew who Jenny was talking about. He had heard everyone talking about the old man named Christopher who sat on the bench and was only present when Jenny was in the group of children. He had no idea why Jenny was saying Christopher's name. His only concern was to get Jenny back to the orphanage. He was chilled from the rain, and he knew that Jenny had to be soaked and cold.

The rain was a slow drizzle by now, but Jake knew he had to get Jenny back into the house and get her warmed up. He checked her arms and legs and nothing seemed to be broken. He wrapped his coat around Jenny and gently picked her up as he talked to her, telling her that he was going to carry her back across the footbridge so they could get into the house and get warm. Jenny did not open her eyes, but put her arm around Jake's neck. Within a few steps, Jake felt her arm go slack. He prayed that she would keep breathing until he got her back to the house.

Jenny was a small child for her age, but Jake was

not a young man and had a hard time carrying her across the playground. He struggled as he walked across the footbridge and had to stop for a minute to catch his breath. Everyone had focused their attention on Miss Cartwright when she fainted, and no one had paid much attention to Jake as he went across the footbridge. As Jake struggled with each step, a couple of people on the other side saw him coming back toward them. They could see he was carrying something and rushed up to help him. By that time, he was more than half way over the footbridge.

When they saw that Jake was carrying Jenny, they were stupefied. It did not take long though for shouts of joy to fill the air. He told them he would carry Jenny the rest of the way. He was not going to relinquish Jenny to anyone. Some of the staff was still looking down the river, and others were standing in awe looking at Jake and Jenny, while others ran to the house to spread the news. Jake yelled for someone to call the doctor.

Jake did not know how Jenny had gotten out of the river and on that bench, just as he did not know who had left her at the gate those many years ago, but he had rescued Jenny once, and he was going to take her to safety again. Jenny did not stir as Jake carried her toward the house. He just prayed over and over that she was not hurt and would be OK.

Miss Cartwright had been revived and had been taken into the house. Everyone else followed Jake and Jenny. The door swung open as Jake walked up on the porch. Mrs. Miller hurried up to Jake as he carried Jenny over the threshold. Her face was grave and all of the color had

Jenny's Angel

drained from it as she saw Jenny in Jake's arms. She was not a person that lost her composure easily, but was almost in a state of shock. How did Jenny fall off the bridge? How did Jake find her? Was she badly hurt? There was total silence as Jake carried Jenny into the room. No one said a word or made a move.

Quickly, Mrs. Miller regained her composure and started barking orders. "Get a pile of blankets, call the doctor, warm some apple cider, get a fire going in the fireplace. Get all the children into dry clothes and bring them around the fire so they can get warm. The rest of you that are wet, change your clothes."

When the news spread that a few of the children had gotten caught in a rain storm on the bridge and that Jenny had fallen into the river, all of the staff had now congregated in the main room. Some were gathered around the windows trying to see what was going on outside, while others were standing in small groups wondering what to do. Others were trying to keep the children calm, which was no easy task. Everyone seemed to be in a state of shock. Upon hearing Mrs. Miller's orders, they quickly gathered their senses and scattered to do as she said. Mrs. Miller was a very kind person, and they all loved her, but they could tell that when she barked those orders, she meant for them to move and move fast!

Mrs. Miller told Jake to take Jenny to her room and lay her down on her bed. Mrs. Miller followed him into Jenny's room. She took Jake's coat from around Jenny, handed it to him and told him to go to his cabin and get some dry clothes on. She saw the concern on Jake's face, but insisted that he go to his cabin and change clothes. He left reluctantly, but she knew he would change clothes as quickly as possible and return to see how Jenny was. He was as concerned about Jenny as she was. She hurriedly shut the door and began to undress Jenny. She wanted to get the wet clothes off, some dry ones on and then get her wrapped in a warm blanket. She prayed that someone had been able to reach Dr. Carlson, and that he was available to come quickly. She knew he would unless he was out on a house call.

Jenny roused a little bit several times and when she did, she mumbled a few words. Mrs. Miller could not understand much of what she was mumbling, but did catch the name Christopher a couple of times. She could not understand why Jenny would be saying his name. She knew that Jenny loved to see the old man and enjoyed taking him a snack, but thought it was rather strange that she kept saying his name.

Mrs. Miller felt Jenny's legs, feet, her arms and hands. She did not seem to have any broken bones. She was not a doctor, but she had seen enough broken limbs in her work with children and could usually tell if one was broken. Jenny did not moan when she touched her which was a good sign. She could see some minor scrapes and bruises beginning to form, but none of them seemed serious. Jenny had a bruise and a good sized lump on her forehead, and that seemed to be the most serious of all. Jenny did flinch as Mrs. Miller gently removed her wet clothes, so that was a good sign too. She was surprised that Jenny felt as warm as she did. Her little cheeks were beginning to regain some of their color which made Mrs. Miller feel optimistic

Jenny's Angel

that Jenny would be OK. This was the second time that a miracle was happening in Jenny's life – the first happened the night Jake discovered the basket at the front gate and now, surviving a fall into the river. Both incidents were surrounded by unimaginable circumstances.

Since Jenny had been miraculously brought out of the river, the fire department was not needed. There were a lot of unexplained events that had taken place in the last hour, and Mrs. Miller had no answers. How did Jenny fall through the slats on the bridge? How did Jenny get out of the river? How did she get to the bench? The answers to these questions would have to wait. Or, would they ever have the answers? Right now all she wanted was to find out if Jenny was OK. She needed to verify that someone had been able to reach Dr. Carlson and find out what he said about coming to the orphanage. She was sure he would come if at all possible. The children in the orphanage seemed to have captured his heart also.

Once Mrs. Miller had Jenny in dry clothes and wrapped in a blanket, she opened the door to find Jake standing right outside, which did not surprise her. He had changed out of his wet clothing and was anxiously waiting for her to open Jenny's door. Mrs. Miller told him to stay with Jenny until she found out if someone had been able to reach Dr. Carlson. Jake told her that Dr. Carlson was on his way. As soon as he had those words out of his mouth, the front door screen slammed, and they could hear the booming voice of Dr. Carlson.

"What happened to Jenny? Where is she? Are the other children OK?"

JENNY'S MIRACLE

He seemed to be extremely upset which was quite unusual for Dr. Carlson. He was always such a gentle person that everyone stopped what they were doing and just stared at him.

"Well," he bellowed, "Don't just stand there. Show me where Jenny is." Everyone jumped into action, and Dr. Carlson was quickly shown the hallway to Jenny's room. He nodded at Jake as he walked by and saw Mrs. Miller standing in the doorway.

The minute Mrs. Miller saw Dr. Carlson, she motioned for him to come into the room and said, "Jenny fell into the river. I have checked her arms and legs, and she does not seem to be hurt except for a few minor scrapes and bruises. She has a nasty bruise and lump on her forehead."

Dr. Carlson looked at Jenny on her bed. Jenny looked like she was sleeping peacefully. As soon as Dr. Carson started his examination of her, Jenny's eyes fluttered and slowly opened. She seemed to be somewhat dazed for a minute and mumbled the name Christopher. She quickly regained her senses and focused in on Dr. Carlson's face. As she recognized him, she gave him a weak smile. Tears welled up in Mrs. Miller's eyes as she let out a gasp. She did not realize that she had been holding her breath as Dr. Carlson began to examine Jenny.

"Well, Jenny," Dr. Carlson said in a gentle voice, "It looks like you took a little swim in the river. Is there anything that hurts?"

Jenny slowly replied to Dr. Carlson that nothing

Jenny's Angel

hurt except her foot hurt a little bit, and her head. Dr. Carlson felt Jenny's crippled foot, turned it as much as he could in each direction and declared that it seemed to be OK. He told Mrs. Miller that Jenny probably twisted it a little bit and that it might be a little sore for a few days.

Dr. Carlson continued to examine Jenny, but did not find anything except for the scrapes and bruises that he was sure would heal in a few days. The pupils in her eyes were of normal size so that was a good thing. He was quite surprised that he did not find anything seriously wrong. If Jenny tumbled off the bridge and fell into the river, she was one lucky little girl that she did not hit her head.

Dr. Carlson wondered how she had gotten out of the river. He knew that the river was very deep and running fast because of the rains that had been falling. Maybe that was a good thing because if she had fallen in when the river was more shallow, she may have landed on a rock and gotten hurt badly.

Dr. Carlson wanted to question Jenny as to how she had gotten out of the river, but thought that it would be best if he left that to Mrs. Miller. He did not know why she had mumbled the name Christopher, but maybe Mrs. Miller would know. Maybe she had a good friend there at the orphanage name Christopher.

Chapter 26

HOME AGAIN

Dr. Carlson patted Jenny's arm and said, "I want to talk to Mrs. Miller for a minute so you stay quiet right here. It won't take long." Jenny nodded her head and seemed to drift off. Dr. Carlson motioned for Mrs. Miller to step into the hall. Jake had stood steadfast in the hallway by the door. He was not going anywhere until he heard what the doctor said. Mrs. Miller assured Jake that Jenny seemed to be OK except for a few scrapes and bruises and for him to go into Jenny's room while she talked to Dr. Carlson. Jake's face broke into a big grin. He was so elated he felt like doing a jig, even if he was too tired.

Dr. Carlson told Mrs. Miller that it looked like Jenny would be just fine, but to keep her rather quiet for the next few days.

"Let her play quietly, but keep her from doing too much running around and playing, even if she says she feels OK. I think she will be just fine, but we want to be cautious for a few days. I will be out again day after tomorrow to check her over. You can always call me if you see anything that worries you. Are the other children alright?"

Mrs. Miller assured Dr. Carlson that she thought the other children were OK. She thought they were just wet and scared, but the staff was taking good care of them. She most certainly would call him if Jenny displayed any symptoms that concerned her, or if any of the other children came

Jenny's Angel

down with anything. As Dr. Carlson started to leave, then turned with a perplexed look on his face and asked Mrs. Miller, "How did Jenny get out of the river? Someone said that Jake found her laying on a bench across the footbridge by the forest."

Mrs. Miller told him that she did not know how Jenny got out of the river. And, yes, Jake found her lying on the bench. It was a mystery to all of them, and they did not have any answers. She explained that Miss Cartwright had taken a few of the children across the footbridge to play, but she had not been able to talk to Miss Cartwright yet to see what had happened. She told him that Miss Cartwright had fainted, but seemed to be feeling alright now. Talking to Miss Cartwright was going to be her next task now that she knew Jenny was OK. Dr. Carlson told her to keep in touch and to be sure to let him know if Jenny displayed any symptoms that he should know about.

As the doctor left, Mrs. Miller went back into Jenny's room. The door was open and she could see Jake sitting in a chair by Jenny's bed. Jenny and Jake were grinning at each other which almost made Mrs. Miller giggle. Jenny seemed to have a way of wrapping people around her little finger, particularly Jake.

As soon as Jenny saw Mrs. Miller, she asked if she could get up and leave her room. Mrs. Miller nodded and told Jake to wait outside until she and Jenny were ready to go out to the big room. She told Jake that she wanted him to carry Jenny. Jake was more than happy to follow those instructions!

HOME AGAIN

Mrs. Miller took a few minutes to pick out some more of the little sticks and leaves that had gotten caught in Jenny's long hair. She tried to brush it a little bit, but it was somewhat of a tangled mess. Oh well, they would work on it again later. She took a cloth and wiped a few smudges of dirt off Jenny's face and arms and declared that she was ready to visit the big room. She wrapped the blanket around Jenny and called for Jake to come in. Jake was elated when he saw Jenny sitting on the edge of her bed. He scooped her up in his arms and carried her to the couch in front of the fireplace where all the other children had gathered. It was not so cold outside that a fire was needed, but a roaring fire in the fireplace always seemed to make everyone cheerful.

When Jake walked into the room carrying Jenny, every one let out a cheer. When they saw Jenny smiling, they all started talking and laughing at once. Jenny started giggling too, and that really made everyone laugh even louder. Even Mrs. Miller let out a hearty laugh. Jake put Jenny on the couch, slapped his leg and yelled "Yahoo!" Even though it had been a near tragedy, everyone now was in a festive mood.

Mrs. Miller called for more hot cider and cookies for everyone. She had totally lost track of time. It might be close to meal time, but she did not care if the children just ate cookies. This was a day for rules to be broken. All of her children were safe, and she was so very thankful.

It took several minutes for the laughter and the chatter to subside. When Mrs. Miller finally got everyone's attention, she told them that due to all that had happened, the next meal would be a little late. Everyone was to gather

Jenny's Angel

in the dining room in an hour if they were hungry. Slowly the staff went back to their jobs, and the children scattered throughout playing games or reading, but Jake hovered over Jenny. He was not going to leave Jenny's side! Mrs. Miller walked over to the couch and told Jake that he could sit with Jenny until she came back. She needed to have a conversation with Miss Cartwright.

Mrs. Miller found Miss Cartwright in the playroom with some of the children. Miss Cartwright looked up as Mrs. Miller walked in and immediately began apologizing for what had taken place on the footbridge. She was afraid that Mrs. Miller was going to be furious with her for endangering the children. Mrs. Miller took her into her office away from the children and told her to calm down. She was not blaming her for what happened. She knew Miss Cartwright was a competent teacher and looked after the children as if she was their mother. She just wanted to find out what really did happen and how Jenny had gotten out of the river.

Miss Cartwright explained how she tried to get the children started across the footbridge when the storm came up so quickly. She had looked back just as Jenny's crutch flew up in the air and she fell through the slats. Jenny had been on the swings and by the time she got off, she was the last one in line. Miss Cartwright said she did not know what to do - go back to where Jenny had been or get the children across the footbridge. Once she thought the children would be OK, she then ran back across and down the footbridge to the edge of the river trying to see what happened to Jenny. She saw Jenny's head bobbing up and down in the water. Miss Cartwright said she knew that she was not a strong swimmer so she did not know whether she should jump in the river or not. Just as she was struggling with what action to take, she saw the old man running down the river bank as he was jerking off his raggedy coat. He threw it down and waded into the river until the water was over his head. She could see both the old man and Jenny bobbing up and down among the debris and rocks. She then ran back across the footbridge. By that time, several of the staff had gathered in the yard. The next thing she knew was she was laying on the ground. When she learned that Jake had found Jenny, she was completely baffled at the whole sequence of events. She could not answer Mrs. Miller's questions about how Jenny got out of the river or how she came to be laying on the bench. She was as puzzled as everyone else. It was just a miracle that Jenny survived.

Mrs. Miller was hoping that Miss Cartwright would have some answers, but she did not know any more than the rest of them. After speaking to her, Mrs. Miller was even more befuddled. Jenny could not have gotten out of that raging river by herself. Jenny had mumbled the old man's name over and over, but there is no way that an old man could have pulled Jenny out of that river. Could he? No, that did not make sense. And even if he did, why would he lay her on the bench and not stay with her. Mrs. Miller believed in miracles, but she was skeptical of one of this magnitude.

Mrs. Miller knew that someone had sent the fire truck back to town, but she had seen the fire chief ambling around talking to different members of the staff when everyone was in the great room. She wanted to talk to him and hoped that he had not left. It did not take long to find

Jenny's Angel

him. There he sat, in the kitchen at the wooden table by the window, with a plate piled high with food. The cooks at the orphanage had quite a reputation for being able to put out a delicious meal, so he was taking the opportunity to avail himself of some of that good cooking.

Mrs. Miller sat down at the table and asked him if he would do a favor for her.

"Of course, I will. What would you like for me to do?"

Mrs. Miller explained that she would like for him to cross the footbridge and look around. Nothing that happened was making any sense to her. She briefly told the fire chief the story that Miss Cartwritght had told her. She expressed that Jenny could not have gotten out of that river by herself, and there was no one around other than the old man that sat on the bench when the children were playing on the playground. She just could not figure any of this out. She did not want to ask any of the staff members to go over today. They had all experienced enough stress for one day, and she did not want to put them through anymore. She was going to try to keep everyone in the house for the rest of the day. The fire chief told Mrs. Miller that as soon as he finished his plate of food, he would be more than happy to go look around.

Mrs. Miller went back to the great room and found Jake still sitting by Jenny's side. She was going to have a hard time getting Jake to leave. Jake told her that Jenny had dozed off a few minutes, but she had been chatting and seemed to feel OK. Mrs. Miller told Jake that he could make

HOME AGAIN

a tray for he and Jenny, and they could eat in the kitchen when Jenny woke up. With a twinkle in his eyes and a big grin, Jake said that he would be delighted to do just that.

Mrs. Miller rang the bell for everyone to gather in the dining room for a late meal. She noticed that the children, and even the staff members, now seemed rather subdued, but she was not surprised. It had been a very nerve-wracking day so she was grateful for the quiet. After making sure that everyone was settled down, she went to the kitchen to make a tray for herself to take to her office. Her stomach was in such an uproar that she was not sure she could eat, but knew that she needed a little something. She also needed some quiet time to mull over all the events of the morning.

Just as Mrs. Miller was finishing her lunch, she looked up to find the fire chief standing in her office doorway. As he walked in, she motioned for him to have a seat. What had he found? She was anxious to hear his report. Maybe he would have some answers for her. She did not know what she expected him to find, but there had to be an answer to what had happened to Jenny.

Chapter 27

THE COAT

Mrs. Miller did not have to ask the fire chief anything. He sat down, shrugged his shoulders and said, "I don't have any answers for you. I looked around the beach and the playground area. I walked down the river bank for several hundred yards. As you know, the river is quite high and flowing rapidly. The only thing I found was an old, raggedy coat that looks like it would fit a rather large man and a long wooden staff. They were laying on the bench, and the coat was soggy. I brought them back and put them on the front porch. The coat looks like it needs to be thrown away, and I don't know why anyone would want the wooden staff. It has some markings on it, but I don't know if they mean anything. Maybe it is a foreign language. I did see a couple of broken slats on the bridge so that must be where Jenny fell through." With a frown on his face, he said, "I did see some very large footprints in the sand and at the edge of the river bank. I thought maybe there were two sets of footprints, one towards the river and one back to the bench, but I could not tell for sure. They could have been there before today. That is all that I can tell you. I wish I had an answer for you."

Mrs. Miller was disappointed that she did not have any of her questions answered. She was still bewildered and was not sure if she was ever going to have any answers. Now there was one more thing to be perplexed about – footprints. Surely those footprints did not mean anything! She thanked the fire chief and as they started to walk out of

THE COAT

her office, there stood Jake with Jenny by his side.

Before any of them could say anything, Jenny said "I heard what you said about that coat and wooden staff. That coat is Christopher's coat, and I have to take it back to him. And, he always had the wooden staff in one hand when he sat on the bench. Please, Mrs. Miller, don't throw Christopher's coat away, or the staff. You have to let me take them back to him."

Mrs. Miller could see that Jenny was becoming very agitated. Dr. Carlson had given instructions to keep her quiet for a couple of days.

"OK, Jenny. Calm down now. We will not throw the coat away. I want you and Mr. Jake to sit down at the table by the window in the kitchen. We will get you a lunch tray, and you can eat in here. Then I want you to go to your room and rest this afternoon for a little while."

Jenny's eyes filled with tears as she pleaded, "Please, I have to take Christopher's coat back to him. Promise me that I can take it back."

Jenny looked up at Jake and cried, "Mr. Jake, will you take me across the footbridge?" Big tears rolled down her cheeks and she sobbed, "Christopher is my special friend."

Mrs. Miller could see that Jenny was getting more and more upset. "Jenny, we will not throw the staff or the coat away. In a few days, when you have rested, Mr. Jake will take you across the footbridge. Now, let Mr. Jake take

Jenny's Angel

you to the table, and he will get something for the two of you to eat. I am sure Mr. Jake is hungry and would like for you to eat with him."

Jenny looked at Mr. Jake and said, "Will you do that Mr. Jake? Will you help me take Christopher's coat to him."

"Of course, I will, little miss. If Mrs. Miller says we can take them back, then we will take them back. But, we have to wait a few days. I am hungry. Let's go eat our lunch." Jake took Jenny by the hand and headed off in the direction of the kitchen. Mrs. Miller and the fire chief walked down the hallway shaking their heads. Who was this Christopher? The fire chief said that he did not know of any elderly man that lived in the forest. No one had ever been able to understand why he only sat on the bench when Jenny was in the group that crossed the footbridge and why she was so attached to him. It was very puzzling.

The next few days passed by uneventfully, much to Mrs. Miller's relief. It took a few days for the conversations to change to a different topic, but there was always something new to talk about around the orphanage. Jenny did not suffer any ill effects from her fall into the river nor were any of the other children traumatized by it. Jenny was the same Jenny, thumping around on her crippled foot and letting out one of her peals of laughter. She had lost one of her shoes in the river so Mrs. Miller had sent a note to the cobbler to ask him if he could make another pair and to her surprise, a pair was delivered within days. The cobbler must have worked night and day to get them done so quickly. Miracles abounded!!

THE COAT

It did not take very many days before Jenny was asking Mrs. Miller if she remembered her promise about Christopher's coat and wooden staff. Mrs. Miller assured Jenny that she had not forgotten, but it would be a few more days. Mrs. Miller told her that none of the children were going across the footbridge for a couple of weeks. Jake was going to fix the wooden slats on the footbridge first, and she wanted to wait until the river had calmed down.

Jenny was not a very patient child in this situation though. Every day she would ask Mrs. Miller if the slats had been fixed, and every day Mrs. Miller would remind her that she had to be patient. No matter how much Mrs. Miller assured Jenny, she worried about taking Christopher's coat and staff back to him, and she needed to take him a cookie. Jenny kept insisting that Christopher would be missing her. Mrs. Miller had hoped that Jenny would forget about the coat and staff, but that was not happening.

Some days, Mrs. Miller would see Jenny standing at the window and look longingly in the direction of the footbridge, or when she was outside, she would walk down the yard to the fence and look in that direction. It did not look like Jenny was going to give up the idea of taking that coat back to the old man.

Mrs. Miller decided that the best way to handle the situation would be to have Jake take Jenny across the bridge and let her put the coat on the bench. She was sure that the old man would not be around anymore, and after a few days, they could show Jenny that he was not going to be back. Then they could discard the coat and staff, and that would be the end of it.

Jenny's Angel

Miss Cartwright indicated she had seen the old man dive into the water, but it was ludicrous to think that he had rescued Jenny from the river and put her on the bench. But, Mrs. Miller did not have a plausible explanation as to how Jenny got on the bench, and there was the strange fact that she was laying on the coat which looked like the one the old man had on every time they saw him. Jenny had miraculously gotten out of the water somehow. She just could not believe that the old man saved Jenny. There was the possibility that the old man had drowned in the raging river. Mrs. Miller knew that her thoughts just were going in circles when she tried to make sense of it all. She wanted answers, but there were none.

When Mrs. Miller told Jenny that Mr. Jake would take her across the footbridge that afternoon, Jenny was elated. Her face lit up with joy, she clapped her hands and twirled around in circles until she fell down. Jenny was always a happy child, but she was absolutely ecstatic with the news. Mrs. Miller told her to go to the dining room to eat lunch and to meet Mr. Jake at the front door at 1:30 p.m.

Chapter 28

RETURNING THE COAT

Jenny scurried off to the dining room, but could hardly eat a bite. She was just too excited. She watched the clock above the doorway, and the minutes seemed to creep by. Instead of eating her two cookies, Jenny carefully wrapped them up in a napkin and put them in her pocket. These cookies would be for Christopher! Finally, she was excused from the dining room table and did not waste any time heading to the front door looking for Mr. Jake.

As Jenny rushed around the corner, she ran right into Miss Cartwright. "Slow down Jenny. Where are you going in such a hurry?" Miss Cartwright asked.

Jenny was breathless. "Oh, Miss Cartwright, Mr. Jake is going to take me across the footbridge, and we are going to take Christopher's coat and staff back to him."

Miss Cartwright smiled and said, "Well, be careful, Jenny. Make sure you hold on to Mr. Jake's hand."

Jenny was much too anxious to get to the front door to have time for any conversation with anyone, even if it was Miss Cartwright, who was her favorite teacher. Just as Jenny got to the front door, Jake was opening the screen door.

"Well, little miss, are you ready to go across the footbridge?"

Jenny's Angel

Jenny looked up at Jake with her big blue eyes shining and said, "Oh yes, Mr. Jake. Let's go. But where is Christopher's coat? We have to take the coat and the wooden staff."

Jake told Jenny that the coat was in a bag on the front porch and the staff was there also. They would pick it up when they went outside. Jenny tugged on his shirt and said, "Let's go Mr. Jake. Let's go right now."

Mrs. Miller was standing at the back of the room watching Jake and Jenny. She was going to be glad when Jake and Jenny made the trip and got back. Maybe then Jenny would forget about the old man!

Jake and Jenny headed across the yard and down the path to the footbridge. Jake carried the staff and the bag with the old raggedy coat with one hand and held Jenny's hand with his other hand. When they got to the footbridge, he certainly was not going to let go of Jenny's hand. The slats had been fixed, and it was a warm, sunny day, but he was not going to take any chances. He was not even going to let her walk close to the edge. He would walk on the side and have her in the middle.

It did not take long to make the trip across the footbridge. They trudged across the sand with Jenny's crippled foot leaving a trail. She had given her crutch to Jake when they started across the sand because it was difficult to use in the sand. Jenny never took her eyes off the bench once it came into sight. Of course, the bench was empty, just as Jake thought it would be.

RETURNING THE COAT

As they approached the bench, Jenny asked Jake to put the staff at the end of the bench and to get the coat out of the bag. He did just as Jenny asked and watched her as she lovingly spread the coat out on the bench. She smoothed out all the wrinkles, folded it one way and then folded it another way. It took Jenny several minutes before she had the coat arranged just the way she wanted it. When she was done, she reached in her pocket and took out the napkin with the two cookies. Jake was astonished at how involved Jenny was in arranging the coat and the cookies.

Jake stood by quietly and did not say a word as Jenny finished her mission. When she was done, she looked at Jake and said, "I know that Christopher will be back to get his staff and coat and the cookies. He has always been my special friend."

Jake still did not say anything to Jenny, because he knew he was not going to convince her of anything about the old man. He asked her if she was ready to go back, and she said that she was. He could tell that she really did not want to leave. Jenny said that she would have to come back in a day or two, though, to see if Christopher had come for his staff and coat and the cookies. She was just sure that he would, but she wanted to come back and check. When Jenny said this, Jake once again did not say anything. He was not sure that Mrs. Miller was going to let them make another trip back across the footbridge for that purpose. He knew Mrs. Miller was hoping that this trip would end Jenny's interest in the old man. He would let Mrs. Miller handle that with Jenny when they got back.

Jenny was happy and chatting on the way back

Jenny's Angel

over the bridge. Once again, Jake held her hand as they crossed. Jenny had her crutch, and she thumped along beside Jake, sometimes breaking into one of the songs she sang in church on Sunday. It never ceased to amaze Jake at what a happy child Jenny was all the time. Sometimes she reminded him of a little tornado of happiness – a whirlwind that drew everyone into her happy world.

As soon as they got over the footbridge, Jenny tugged on Jake's hand to hurry so they could find Mrs. Miller and talk to her about going back in a day or two. Jake was reluctant to go with her, but he knew it would be of no use to try to dissuade her. She had never wavered in her loyalty to the old man.

Jenny looked up at Jake with those big, blue eyes with a worried look on her face and pleaded, "Mr. Jake, please, you need to go with me to talk to Mrs. Miller. I have to go back across the footbridge, and she will want you to go with me. Please, Mr. Jake."

How could Jake resist Jenny? He could never say no so off they went to find Mrs. Miller. He was not looking forward to the conversation, and as he expected, it did not go well. Mrs. Miller did everything she could to try to convince Jenny that it was not necessary to go back in a day or two. Jenny could not be persuaded. What was this strange attachment that Jenny had to this old man?

After much pleading and cajoling on Jenny's part, Mrs. Miller told her that if Mr. Jake had time in a couple of days, they could make one more trip back over the footbridge, but Jenny had to promise that she would not ask to go back again except when all the children went over to play. She also must be patient and wait for a time that Mr. Jake had his work done and could take her. Mrs. Miller reminded her that there would not be too many more trips because school was getting ready to start and cold weather would be coming.

Jenny jumped up and down when Mrs. Miller finally relented to one more trip and said, "Oh, I promise, I promise, Mrs. Miller. If you let Mr. Jake take me across one more time, I will not ask again. And, I will be patient, but I hope it is soon. I just know that Christopher is going to come back for his coat and staff. I know that he is close by. I just know it."

Mrs. Miller and Jake just looked at each other. The whole episode with Jenny falling in the river had been very strange. No one had ever figured out how Jenny had gotten out of the river and on that bench with an old coat beneath her. They just could not believe that the old man had rescued Jenny, but that is what she kept insisting. He was very old, and if he had rescued Jenny, why did he put her on the bench and leave? Why didn't he bring her to the orphanage? No, her story was just impossible to believe. But, even with all the rationalizing, they still could not come up with a feasible answer of how Jenny got out of the river unhurt and on that bench. There had to be a logical answer, but what was it? Would they ever know?

Chapter 29

THE MEDALLION

A couple of days later, Jake went looking for Jenny and found her sitting on the sofa reading a book. When she saw him, her eyes lit up.

"Hi, Mr. Jake. What are you doing?"

Jake walked over and keeled down by the sofa and said, "I have some extra time right now, and I have asked Mrs. Miller if you and I could make our last trip across the footbridge. She said OK, so if you get your shoes on and your crutch, we will go."

Jenny was off that sofa in a flash and sat on the floor to put her shoes on. She grabbed her crutch and Jake's hand and said, "Let's go, Mr. Jake. But first, I have to go to the kitchen and see if somebody will give me a couple of cookies to take to Christopher. I always take Christopher something to eat. Please wait right here for me."

Before Jake could say another word, Jenny dashed off toward the kitchen. It did not take long before she was back with the cookies wrapped safely in a couple of napkins and safely secured in her pocket.

"OK, Mr. Jake. Let's go across the footbridge."

So, off they went scurrying through the yard to the base of the footbridge. Jenny tugged on Jake's sleeve to walk

THE MEDALLION

faster. Jake grabbed Jenny's hand as they started across and held it until they got to the other side. As soon as they got off the footbridge, Jenny pulled loose from Jake's hand and scrambled through the sand and playground area and up to the bench.

"Hurry, Mr. Jake. Look. Come see. Christopher's coat is gone. And look, the wooden staff is gone too. I knew he would come for his coat and staff and for the cookies I left for him. And, Mr. Jake, look. There is a piece of paper here with my name on it. I think Christopher wrote me a note."

Jake was astounded to find that both the staff and the coat were gone, the cookies were also gone and, yes, there was a piece of paper that had been folded several times. It was lying on the bench so you could see Jenny's name written in bold letters. His first thought, was what happened to the coat and staff? They could not have been carried off by an animal. The cookies could have been eaten by birds, but he would not be able to convince Jenny of that. And, how did that folded piece of paper get on the bench with Jenny's name on it?

Jenny was beaming as she looked up at Jake. Her big, round eyes were the deepest blue he had ever seen, and her smile would have lit up a room. She was ecstatic. Jake did not know what to think. He was totally baffled, but there was nothing to do except unfold the paper and see if there was something written on the inside.

"Well, Jenny, I guess since it has your name on it, then you should open it and read it. Jenny carefully picked

Jenny's Angel

the paper up and held it for a few seconds. She looked up at Jake with a slight frown and said, "It feels like there is something folded up inside of this paper. It is hard. Maybe you should open it."

Jake took the paper from Jenny's hand and felt it. He could not imagine what was inside, but there was definitely something small and hard wrapped inside the paper. As he unfolded the paper, a medallion fell to the ground. Both he and Jenny looked at it in amazement. Jenny gently picked up the medallion and studied it. Jake did not say a word as she looked at one side and then at the other, turning it back and forth several times.

Finally, Jenny looked up with a glow on her face and said, "It has writing on it. I think it says St. Christopher. Is that right, Mr. Jake?"

Jake was speechless. Jenny was holding a St. Christopher's medal!

Jenny opened the paper. There was a note written in large, bold, black letters. Slowly Jenny read the note out loud to Jake.

"Wherever you go, Jenny, I will always be there for you."

Jake did not say a word. He was too stunned! All he could do was wonder who wrote that note and put it on the bench. He could rationalize that the coat and staff had been carried away by animals, but there was no explanation for this note and the medallion. Now more questions were

THE MEDALLION

being created!

Jenny looked up at Jake, then at the note and then toward the forest. She stood without moving a muscle staring into the forest of trees. Jake did not make a sound. After what seemed like an eternity to Jake, Jenny's face broke out into a grin and she giggled. Her face was aglow with happiness.

Jenny pointed toward the forest and excitedly said, "Mr. Jake, I can see Christopher. He is waving to me."

Jake could not believe what Jenny was saying. He looked in the direction to where Jenny was pointing. All he could see was a forest of trees. Jenny had always had a big imagination, but this was ridiculous. Jake was beginning to be anxious to get back to the orphanage. He looked back at Jenny to tell her that there was no one there, but the look of pure joy on her face made him change his mind. No one had ever been able to convince her of anything concerning the old man, and he was sure that he was not going to be able to convince her now.

Jenny looked back at Jake and said in a very serious tone, "Christopher whispered to me that my foot is going to get better, and that soon I will not need a crutch. He said not to worry about him."

After hearing this, Jake was determined to get Jenny back to the orphanage a quickly as possible. Mrs. Miller is not going to believe what Jake had to tell her.

Jake did not want to upset Jenny so he tried to stay

Jenny's Angel

calm and not let his frustration show. He told Jenny that it was time to get back to the orphanage. Jenny took one last look at the forest with a big dimpled smile and raised her hand in a wave. She tucked the medallion and note in her pocket and grabbed Jake's hand and said, "OK, Mr. Jake. I am ready to make the trip back across the footbridge."

When Jake and Jenny return to the house, Jenny looked up at Jake. "Thank you, Mr. Jake, for taking me to take Christopher's coat and staff back to him. I know he will need it so that he will be warm this winter. I remember exactly what he said to me."

Jenny squeezed Jake's hand and ran off toward the play room, dragging her crutch before Jake had time to say a word. Jake was shocked at Jenny's attitude. She did not seem upset or anxious. She did not mention going back to see Christopher. She did not mention her crippled foot. All Jake could think of was to find Mrs. Miller as quickly as possible.

It did not take Jake long to find Mrs. Miller and relate what had taken place. Mrs. Miller made him tell it to her several times. She just sat listening with a frown on her face. After repeating every little detail as best he could remember, Mrs. Miller said, "Well, Jake, at least Jenny did not come flying into the house wanting to know when she was going to get to go back over the footbridge to see the old man. Maybe now Jenny is satisfied. I wish we had answers to all of this. The only thing that concerns me is that she thinks her foot is going to get better. I do not want her to be disappointed. I guess we will deal with that problem as it comes up. Thank you for being so patient with Jenny."

THE MEDALLION

When Mrs. Miller was able to carve out some time alone, she sat at her desk and mulled over what Jake had told her. Jake had said that Jenny told him she saw Christopher in the forest, and he whispered in her ear. One of the things he told her was that her foot was going to be healed. Why would Jenny say that? And, now Jenny was content not to go back across the footbridge to see the old man. This was a complete change in her attitude from the last several weeks. Where did the note come from? Where did the medallion come from? Jenny's life seemed to be filled with miracles, but all of this was just too much. Mrs. Miller knew that she had even entertained the idea that Jenny's foot might straighten out someday, but that was more wishful thinking than anything else. She could not make any sense of any of it starting with the first day Jenny saw the old man on the bench until today. It was all a mystery.

Mrs. Miller was very busy over the next few days getting ready for the school year to start, and she kept Jake busy building new shelves in one of the classrooms, cleaning and a multitude of other tasks. Jenny was busy playing with the other children and working on her projects. She never approached either of them about making more trips across the footbridge or even mentioned Christopher. Occasionally, Mrs. Miller would observe Jenny rubbing her foot. She wondered if it hurt, or if Jenny was thinking about the old man telling her it was going to be healed someday. Mrs. Miller did not want to bring the subject up to Jenny. Several days later after lunch, Mrs. Miller walked down the hallway to her office. As she approached the door she could see a little crutch leaning against the wall by the door. As she got closer, she could see that a piece of paper was tied onto the crutch with a piece of red ribbon. She

Jenny's Angel

immediately thought of Jenny because Jenny was the only one of the children that was using a crutch at this time. Her heart lurched and began beating faster. She was baffled at why Jenny would leave her crutch at her doorway.

Carefully Mrs. Miller untied the bow and pulled the ribbon. The note was a little scrunched after being tied with the ribbon. As she unfolded it, she saw that it was decorated with red hearts all around the edges. In the middle was a big heart, and in the middle of the heart was a message written in a child's handwriting.

"I will not need this anymore. Jenny."

Chapter 30

ANOTHER MIRACLE

What was Jenny talking about? What was she thinking? Nothing had been the same with Jenny since she first saw the old man, Christopher. She was still the happy, delightful child, but Mrs. Miller never knew for sure what Jenny was going to come up with.

She immediately grabbed the crutch and turned back down the hall looking for Jake. Maybe he knew something about what was going on with Jenny. After checking several classrooms, she found Jake working on a shelving unit. She showed the note and crutch to him. Seeing the concern on Mrs. Miller's face made Jake apprehensive. What was she doing with Jenny's crutch? Had something happened to Jenny? He carefully unfolded the note and read it out loud. Jake shrugged his shoulders and said, "I think we need to find Jenny and find out why she wrote this note."

Finding Jenny was not a difficult task. All you had to do was follow the sound of laughter, and you could find Jenny. When she saw Mrs. Miller and Jake, she ran toward them – no thumping, no limping, two feet pointed in the same direction!

Mrs. Miller and Jake did not take another step or say a word, but simply stared at Jenny as she ran towards them. They were frozen in their tracks.

Jenny threw her arms around both of them, ran in a

Jenny's Angel

circle around them and immediately ran back to the other children. Then she turned toward them and let out one of her famous squeals. Neither Mrs. Miller nor Jake could say a word!

Jenny walked back to them and said, "My foot is not crippled. I can run and jump and play. Christopher told me it would be healed."

How could either of them argue with Jenny? They could see it with their own eyes.

Had another miracle occurred in Jenny's life? There was no explanation.

A few days later Dr. Carlson made one of his routine stops at the orphanage to check on the children. Mrs. Miller saw him as he came in and immediately asked Dr. Carlson to stop by her office before leaving the building. She was quite anxious to talk to him about Jenny. He was never going to believe what she had to tell him!

The minute Dr. Carlson opened the door, Mrs. Miller started rattling off what she and Jake had observed. Dr. Carlson had never seen Mrs. Miller so flustered. She was talking so fast that Dr. Carlson was having a very difficult time making out what she was saying, but he finally determined that it was about Jenny. He sat down in the chair by the desk and asked Mrs. Miller to start all over with her story and try to calm down.

Suddenly, the sound of laughter could be heard and the office door burst open. Mrs. Miller and Dr. Carlson

ANOTHER MIRACLE

quickly looked to see who was barging into the office. No one ever opened Mrs. Miller's door without first knocking.

There Jake and Jenny stood in the doorway. Jenny's face was beaming. She ran across the room to Dr. Carlson and jumped into his lap before he had a chance to stand up. She wrapped her arms around his neck and exclaimed, "Look, Dr. Carlson, Christopher fixed my foot."

Jake and Mrs. Miller did not make a sound as Dr. Carlson put his arms around Jenny and held her tightly. Finally Jenny loosened her grip from his neck and wiggled away. She jumped off his lap and did a little dance in the middle of the room, giggling and chanting, "Watch me dance, watch me dance." It was a magical moment and Jake, Mrs. Miller and Dr. Carlson stood silently watching with big grins on their face. What else could they do?

Dr. Carlson grabbed Jenny's hand and did a little dance with her. Jake and Mrs. Miller let out a whoop and a laugh that could probably have been heard all over the orphanage. It did not take long before Dr. Carlson was out of breath. He held on to Jenny's hand and walked her around to Mrs. Miller's padded office chair. He sat her in it, pulled another chair up close and said, "Jenny, is it OK if we take your shoe and sock off so I can take a look at your foot?"

Jenny was grinning from ear to ear as she said, "Sure. I want you to see it. It is perfect. I knew it was going to be perfect someday."

She held her leg out and Dr. Carlson propped it on

his knee as he removed Jenny's shoe and sock. Mrs. Miller and Jake moved closer in so they could see Jenny's foot as the sock was removed. They certainly were not looking at it for the first time, but they never got tired of seeing that one crippled foot perfectly formed. Dr. Carlson prodded Jenny's ankle and moved it in every direction. Nobody said a word! As he examined Jenny's foot, you could see a tear running down his cheek.

Dr. Carlson finally looked up at Mrs. Miller and Jake and proclaimed, "Jenny's foot and ankle are perfect. As a doctor, I have had the good fortune to see medicine do many wonderful things, but it is not often that we have the privilege of seeing a miracle."

With her voice full of emotion, Mrs. Miller exclaimed, "How blessed we are. We now have had that privilege of seeing another one of God's miracles."

As Jake stood staring at his Jenny, he was so overcome with emotion that he could not utter a word. Tears welled up in his eyes and his lips quivered as they broke out into a broad grin.

"In my career as a doctor, I have seen many wonderful and unexpected occurrences. Medicine can do some wonderful things but only God can work miracles. This is truly a miracle from God."

With her sock and shoe still lying on the floor, Jenny jumped out of the chair and ran to each of them, throwing her arms around their waists while she let out one of her famous giggles. Tears of happiness ran down their cheeks.

Chapter 31

GROWING UP

Jenny continued to stay at the orphanage even though several families had offered to adopt her. She was an intelligent, well-mannered, beautiful child, but Jenny did not want to leave the orphanage. Mrs. Miller and Jake were secretly delighted each time Jenny expressed her desire to stay, although they never discussed their feelings.

When Jenny reached what would have been classified as her freshman year in high school, she was sent to the local high school along with a few other children that had not been adopted. The group was very small as most all the children at Anderson Calvary Orphanage were adopted out long before they became that age. Jake would take all of them into town every morning and pick them up after school.

During the four years of high school, Jenny blossomed into a beautiful, blue eyed young lady whom all the boys were interested in escorting to the high school dances and games. She excelled in her studies and became involved in many of the school activities. Just as when she was younger, she was oblivious to her beauty and her magnetic personality.

As she matured, Jenny never lost her love for the "Littles" at the orphanage. She helped them with their homework, sat with them during mealtime and gave special attention to any little boy or girl that had a physical deformity. She could soothe their hurt feelings and make them feel special. Jenny had a special touch and could calm a crying child when no one else could get the job done.

Jenny spent many hours talking to Mrs. Miller about how she wanted to be a teacher and teach at the orphanage. Mrs. Miller remembered Jenny as a little girl gathering the other children around her, telling them stories and reading to them. At that time, she never dreamed that this was a precursor to Jenny's future desires.

Mrs. Miller never discouraged Jenny's conversations, nor did she discourage her desire to be a teacher at the orphanage. She thought that as Jenny matured and was exposed to other areas in her schooling, she would change her mind, but that never happened. Jenny stood steadfast in her decision to become a teacher and return to the orphanage. Her only reluctance was that she would need to leave the orphanage to go to college. She fretted about this quite often.

With the help of the school counselor and Mrs. Miller, it was arranged for Jenny to go to a teacher's college nearby. Mrs. Miller never knew just exactly where the money came from to pay for Jenny's college education, but she often suspected that Dr. Carlson was the benefactor and had arranged for it through the school counselor.

Jenny was thrilled at the chance to go to that particular teacher's college as it was close enough for her to return to the orphanage for the holidays and during the summer. She insisted on working at the orphanage during the summer doing whatever they needed her to do to pay for her room and board. Jenny received her teaching certificate in record time by doubling up on classes and returned as a teacher in just two and a half years.

Jake was quite an elderly man by the time Jenny went to college, but he never hesitated to make the trips between the orphanage and the college to pick Jenny up. He did not have many duties at the orphanage, but he was such an integral part of it that no one expected him to leave. No matter how old Jenny was, she was his special little girl. After every trip, he would sit in his rocking chair and re-live the time he found Jenny in the basket at the gate, the trips over the bridge to the playground, the time Jenny fell off the bridge, and the healing of her foot. Each one of them was a miracle!

Chapter 32

THE PASSING YEARS

Throughout the years, Mrs. Miller and Jake became quite good friends. The orphanage was their mission in life which gave them a common bond, not to mention the events that had taken place in Jenny's life. These events affected everyone at the orphanage, but not like Mrs. Miller and Jake.

Mrs. Miller was always in awe of how the orphanage continued to receive the necessary funding to keep it functioning. Mr. Anderson had left a great deal of money for the creation and operation of the orphanage, but over the years, the funds began to be depleted. Just when she would get concerned, another miracle in the form of donations would be received. She was thrilled when visitors would come bearing monetary gifts only to learn that they had once been residents for a period of time in their childhood. This was a testimony that not only had they received the emotional support they needed, but they had also received a proper education which enabled them to have a successful life. One such former resident became so successful he donated enough money to refurbish the entire structure and add a few more bedrooms, thereby allowing for the care of even more children.

Jenny began her teaching career in the kindergarten class and throughout the years, taught every grade, but her heart was always with the "Littles." She was Miss Jenny to all the children. As Mrs. Miller watched Jenny work with

THE PASSING YEARS

the children, she knew who the perfect person would be to step into her shoes when the time came – Jenny! She began grooming Jenny for the job without Jenny even being aware of it.

When Miss Jenny received her first paycheck as a teacher at the orphanage, she put part of it in a special envelope marked "Christopher's Footbridge and Bench." Every paycheck, a little more money would be tucked into that envelope. She wanted to make sure that funds would always be available for any needed repairs, or if funds were needed for a special pair of shoes for another little boy or girl.

The image of Christopher sitting on the bench in his raggedy coat was a vision that never dimmed in her mind. It was an important part of her life at the orphanage and would never be forgotten. She even had Jake make two signs – Christopher's Footbridge and Christopher's Bench – which were secured into the ground. These signs often elicited questions from her students, and she told the story of her "miracle foot" over and over. The children would sit around her with their upturned faces hanging onto every word she said. Miss Jenny wanted each child to believe in God's miracles!

Upon Mrs. Miller's retirement, Miss Jenny was made the director of the Anderson Calvary Orphanage. With Jake and Mrs. Miller at her side, it was as though her life was complete. She knew immediately that their mission had become her mission in life. Miss Jenny started life as a tiny baby in the Anderson Calvary Orphanage, and her life would someday end in that very orphanage.

Jenny's Angel

As the years passed, Miss Jenny never wavered in her decision to become a teacher. The only incidents that marred her life were the deaths of the two people she loved most – Mrs. Miller, her life long friend and mentor and Mr. Jake with whom she had a very special bond.

Because of her dedication throughout the years, as Miss Jenny declined in age and was no longer able to continue as the director of Anderson Calvary Orphanage, she was provided with comfortable quarters. She continued to visit each classroom every day and delight the children with her presence. As Miss Jenny aged, she never lost the infectious laugh that she had as a child, which made all of the children giggle. They loved her as much as she loved them.

Quite often, Miss Jenny would sit quietly in her rocking chair during the evening hours with a book open in her lap, but never turned a page. She would stare off into space with a hint of a smile on her face, and quite often would take a chain from around her neck. Miss Jenny always wore the chain with the medallion on it. She would look at the medallion and gently rub her fingers across it. If you got close enough, you could hear her whisper, "My friend, Christopher."

Throughout the years, Miss Jenny took the children across the footbridge to the playground. These trips did not stop when she retired as director. The older she got, the more important these treks across the bridge seemed to be. There was no one left at the orphanage that remembered Jenny's fall into the Calvary River so there was no one that could fully understood why that footbridge and bench were

THE PASSING YEARS

so important to her. Often times, she was content to sit on the bench with the sun shining on her face.

Chapter 33

ONE LAST VISIT

One warm summer day when there was not a cloud in the sky, Miss Jenny requested that one of the staff members walk across the footbridge with her. Miss Jenny had always insisted on going by herself. At those times, one of the staff members would watch as Miss Jenny walked across the footbridge to make sure she was safe. She would sit on the bench while the staff member busied herself in the yard waiting for her to return.

All the staff members loved Jenny so it was not hard to find a volunteer to walk across the bridge. Miss Jenny and Rosa, a staff member, slowly walked down through the yard. As they approached the bridge, Jenny stood before the sign "Christopher's Bridge" for several minutes. Rosa waited for Miss Jenny to cross the footbridge and walked slowly beside her. When they approached the bench, Miss Jenny stopped once again to look at the sign that said "Christopher's Bench." She looked at Rosa and said that she would like to be alone for a few minutes. Rosa walked over to one of the swings on the playground and sat down in it. As she did, she saw Miss Jenny sit down and pull a napkin out of her pocket. She unwrapped a cookie and then wrapped it back in the napkin. She turned it over and over in her hands and finally set it down on the bench beside her.

A gentle breeze ruffled Jenny's snow white curls as she sat on the bench. Her face was aglow as though she was the happiest person on earth and a giggled escaped.

ONE LAST VISIT

Jenny was fingering the medallion around her neck. Rosa watched Jenny closely and saw her lips begin to move.

There were no other sounds but Miss Jenny's voice, and she heard Miss Jenny say, "Hello, Christopher. You were my Special Angel. Even though our time together was many decades ago, I have never forgotten you."

Rosa had many times heard the story of Miss Jenny's plunge into the river, her miraculous escape, and the healing of her foot. Even so, she was surprised at Miss Jenny's words. Rosa never took her eyes off Miss Jenny as she sat on the bench for several minutes. She saw Miss Jenny smile, raise her face to heaven, her face aglow with happiness. Miss Jenny slowly removed her sweater, placed it at the end of the bench and gently lowered her body with her head resting on her sweater. As she did this, Rosa heard her say, "Christopher, my Special Friend and Angel."

Alarmed, Rosa walked over to the bench and saw that Jenny's eyes were closed, but the smile had not faded. The St. Christopher's medallion rested in her hand. Rosa knew that Jenny had breathed her last breath in the presence of her Angel, Christopher.

The End